BRISTOL

Last Age of the Merchant Princes

Tim Mowl with photographs by Chris Bland

Millstream Books

To Reg Redwood –
last of those Edwardians who succeeded the Fosters,
who in their turn succeeded the Patys
and who together raised Ruskin's city

First published 1991
Millstream Books, 7 Orange Grove, Bath BA1 1LP
Composed in Janson Text by Ryburn Typesetting Ltd, Halifax
Printed in Great Britain by The Amadeus Press, Huddersfield
© Tim Mowl and Chris Bland
ISBN   0 948975 25 3

Front cover illustration: The Granary, Welsh Back (see plate 41)
Back cover illustration: Christ Church, Clifton (see plate 11)

Preface

The purpose of this book is to celebrate the extraordinary richness of architecture in Bristol of the period 1837–1910. It is not meant to be a comprehensive gazetteer of everything built in the city during those two self-confident reigns, more a personal selection of those buildings which I felt deserved attention. As such it is highly personal in its opinions, though I have always tried to keep my enthusiasms within sensible bounds. However, the writing of it has come as an aesthetic shock to my system. John Betjeman has always been my hero, but I remained sceptical about Victoriana. That was until I bought an early Victorian town house in Cotham and began to write the following descriptions.

Being a Georgian groupie I had been shackled for too long in the straitjacket of 18th-century formalism, so these excursions into the following century were exhilarating. Victorian architects could and would achieve the most dazzling effects without thinking twice. There seemed to be no rules, no constraints, no prissy good taste. As a consequence I have been shaken up at just the point when my aesthetic sensibilities were beginning to stagnate.

Not only has the writing of this book made me more visually aware of what seemed an alien century, it has opened up areas of Bristol I never knew existed. The major influence on my selection has been Andor Gomme whose section on this period in *Bristol: an Architectural History* and his street index of buildings of interest are both masterly. He is one of the most searching of architectural writers, rarely inaccurate in his facts, though I would question his judgement of William Venn Gough. But then Gough is an exciting rogue with whom I instinctively sympathise. As a visual and historical record of Bristol's 19th-century architecture, Clare Crick's *Victorian Buildings in Bristol* is without equal. There I saw pinnacles that had been bomb-blasted, decoration that came so costly it was shelved and buildings that were projected but which never materialised.

Credit for my geographical orientation must go to Stewart Harding who, over pints of beer in Fishponds, pestered me into going out to see the threatened Greenbank Cemetery Chapels, the improbable palace of the Glenside Hospital and his own workplace, St Matthias College. He has also answered my many queries about the still-sketchy and seemingly limitless suburbs of north Bristol.

Almost everyone I approached was helpful in some way or another, but I would like to make special mention of the following: Mr Phillips at the Air Balloon Schools who set me onto the architects of the buildings and a useful contemporary newspaper report; Richard Pedlar, architect to Blagden Packaging, who showed me copies of the original drawings by Milverton Drake for that Ruritanian castle; John Williams and his staff at the Record Office where I consulted the near-crumbling architects' plans in the City Engineer's Building Grant volumes; the staff of the Public Library where I sat in the stacks browsing the *Builder*; Mike Hill who walked the streets with me one freezing January day and put me right on the Arts and Crafts; my wife Wendy who handled the complexities of the word processor for me with terrifying precision; and last, but not least, my usual co-author, Brian Earnshaw, who gave his support, encouragement and his typically argumentative insights.

But the ultimate success of a book like this depends to a large extent upon its photographs, and I had the good fortune to find Chris Bland who must be one of the best of current architectural photographers. Not only did he take pictures to precisely my requirements, but he opened my eyes to elements of buildings I thought I knew well with his subtle nuances of angle and approach. On his behalf I should like to thank all those people who let him out onto their balconies, into their upstairs rooms, watched anxiously while he set up ladders on their walls and cheerfully endured the glare of his halogen lights. Through this preface he would like to thank his wife, Susi, for her invaluable support and her lost weekends.

Finally my thanks must go to Tim Graham at Millstream Books in Bath who had the insight to commission a book on a rival city, and who has dealt with all the ups and downs in his invariably professional and phlegmatic style.

Tim Mowl, Cotham, Spring 1991

A Prophet for the Princes

Bristol was John Ruskin's city. Its history, the sequence of its prosperity and even the polychromatic potential of its rocks made it more vulnerable to the lilting prose of *The Seven Lamps of Architecture* and *The Stones of Venice* than other major British industrial centres. Then there was the Avon and the Floating Harbour, a wasting asset but still busy with shipping and allowing the city to feel at least a third cousinship with Venice and its lagoon. Bristol had the sea at a discreet distance, without storms or tidal surges, a romantic mercantile past, and there was, thanks to Clifton, a large educated bourgeoisie, people of Ruskin's class, to appreciate art, architecture and the reactionary romanticism that Ruskin preached so seductively: "The fact is, there are only two fine arts possible to the human race, sculpture and painting. What we call architecture is only the association of these in noble masses, or the placing of them in fit places. All architecture other than this is, in fact, mere building."

As the 1850s opened, villas in the 'Grecian Style' were rising around Durdham Down and classical terraces on the grandest scale – Vyvyan, Worcester, Burlington and Aberdeen; but by the end of the decade pointed arches and pinnacles had stormed residential streets, business premises and warehouses all over the city. The Ruskinian conversion had been swift and complete.

What it produced is still undervalued though the pace of philistine destruction has slackened. St Mary Redcliffe and the Cathedral choir have always been appreciated and Clifton praised for the accident of bold building on a dramatic natural site. But Bristol's real architectural treasure is its business 'square mile': an extraordinary compression, part 18th-century, but largely an eclectic richness of Victorian and Edwardian buildings all attempting wildly to outface each other, clashing in style, often outrageous in ornament. There are domes, spires, pinnacles, statuary, pilastrades and colonnades from Italy, France, Flanders and, latterly, 17th and 18th-century England; but all transmuted by a concentration of wealth, a distortion of function and the unavoidable verticality of a crowded street scene. What 19th-century London, capital of a rich empire, once was, Bristol still is. With luck, its business centre will survive to become in the next century a tourist's prodigy like 16th-century Lavenham, 18th-century Edinburgh or mediaeval Bruges.

The turning point when neo-Classicism, apparently so healthy, suddenly gave up the ghost, came in 1854. In that year the Bristol Society of Architects appeared to be completely in the hands of the old gang, men like R S Pope who had designed the Irvingite church (St Mary on the Quay) and the Royal Western Hotel (Brunel House) as if there were no Gothic tomorrow. The most rigid and rectangular classicist of them all, Charles Underwood, was the Society's chairman and a natural, therefore, to design a home for the West of England Academy facing the Victoria Rooms. He was, inevitably, chosen yet deliberately stepped back to take J H Hirst as his partner and as the actual designer of the Academy. This was because he sensed that classicism was clapped out and the eclectic tide was running. Hirst's Italianate solution is literally a frame for sculpture, a resounding response to Ruskin's: "I believe the right question to ask, respecting all ornament, is simply this: Was it done with enjoyment – was the carver happy while he was about it? It may be the hardest work possible, and the harder because so much pleasure was taken in it; but it must have been happy too, or it will not be living."

Bristol gave up the Gothic Revival of native English architecture the more readily because its own version, buildings like Temple Meads Station and Queen Elizabeth's Hospital, were repetitive, uninspiring examples of Ruskin's "detestable Perpendicular". They possessed none of the Gothic qualities: depth, diversity and natural forms, "leaves which, under the Italian's hand, roll, and flow, and bow down over their black shadows, as in the wearyness of noon-day heat", that delighted Ruskin.

But Bristol was soon to have them all, and more besides. The city seems never, like Chester, to have looked back to its own mediaeval past for inspiration. Instead Bristol architects, always an insular tribe, protective of their patch and mistrustful of outsiders, looked to the *Builder*, edited from 1844 to 1883 by George Godwin, and tried their hand at what they saw on its pages.

An extraordinary period began, when it was not precisely the style or source of a building that mattered, and certainly not its functional efficiency, but its spiritual and aesthetic qualities, the extent to which it responded to Ruskin's rhapsodic requirements. He had stated, "a man who has the gift will take up any style that is going" and "it does not matter one marble splinter whether we have an old or new architecture", so long, however, as that architecture was not Georgian. Renaissance architecture had been "the school which has conducted men's inventive and constructive faculties from the Grand Canal to Gower Street; from the marble shaft, and the lancet arch, and the wreathed leafage, and the glowing and melting harmony of gold and azure, to the square cavity in the brick wall."

With such mystic directions it is fascinating to see how Bristol's architects fanned out from the neo-Classical practice that had satisfied them and their fathers. Where the Royal Promenade in Victoria Square had seemed so daring with its round-arched classicism a few years before, John Yalland now pitched headlong into the Rundbogenstil in 1855 with the south-west range of the same square, in hot red stone. Renaissance certainly, but Venetian and biforate enough to escape the curse of the "square cavity in the brick wall". A year before, in 1854, William Bruce Gingell had taken an even more public Venetian plunge with his West of England and South Wales Bank. This is an astonishing building that still makes a walk along Corn Street an architectural pilgrimage and a delight. Ruskin had written five years before: "I do not believe that ever any building was truly great, unless it had mighty masses, vigorous and deep, of shadow mingled with its surfaces. And among the first habits that a young architect should learn, is that of thinking in shadow … Let him cut out the shadows, as men dig wells in unwatered places." Gingell certainly dug deep and it is an experience that few cities afford to turn the corner into Broad Street and enjoy Charles Cockerell's comparable yet wholly contrasted exercise in the same masonry of shade.

Made bold by their successful experiments in the Italian renaissance and urged on by another Godwin, Edward William, the chairman of their Society, Bristol architects pushed out into the even more rewarding and truly Ruskinian areas of Italian mediaevalism. The Museum and Library (University Refectory) at the top of Park Street by Foster and Ponton, The Granary on Welsh Back by Ponton and Gough, and the Avon Insurance Building in Broad Street, again by Ponton, represent the first great age of the Merchant Princes' confidence, when capitalism believed that gain and the spirit could and should go hand in hand.

All these were of the 1860s, the flowering time also of the 'Bristol Byzantine', that sub-style which has caught the imagination by its alliterative assault, but which has left little of importance. Afficionados of the style should hunt down a domestic version of the same Romanesque, richer in carved detail and therefore more Ruskinian, in Pembroke Road which, with its adjoining streets, totally outpoints North Oxford for invention and applied workmanship.

It is impossible to call Bristol's architecture of the '70s and '80s dull, if only because William Venn Gough, the city's home-bred Butterfield, was active in them. But generally there was a fading of the earlier fire. The mannered predictabilities of French and Flemish forms of the 16th and 17th centuries are a poor substitute for that wrestling with the intractable Middle Ages.

Then, as the influence of Ruskin led naturally to the Pre-Raphaelites and William Morris, vitality and experiment surged back. Designers recovered their eclectic nerve. English classicism was no longer a forbidden area when Edward Gabriel could create a dynamic five-storey block for the London and Lancashire Assurance on Corn Street by heaping up diverse elements from as many native country houses. The literary link with aesthetic polemics had already been established when the printer, Edward Everard, commissioned Henry Williams in 1900 to work with the tiler, W J Neatby, and evoke on Broad Street the colourful, ideal world of socialist labour in Morris's *News from Nowhere*.

There is a pervading optimism to Edwardian design in the city, eclectic still, but with a new satisfaction in the English past exemplified in the serene rotunda that Oatley and Lawrence devised for the Scottish Provident Building on Clare Street. For the patronage behind all this architectural advance was essentially commercial, capitalist, acquisitive. There were exceptions like Holden's Municipal Library, but the roots are in the mud of the harbour, colliery and brass foundry.

Across the river on St Philip's Marsh, wreathed at that time in the smoke of 20 active industries, was the St Vincent's Ironworks of John Lysaght Ltd. Though grandly named, Lysaght's produced corrugated iron sheets and cheap metal buckets, but still thought it natural to give their new offices of 1891 the exterior of a dream-like Norman castle and an interior fantasy of a domed Italian palace. By such a gesture Merchant Princes earn that title. Structures like Lysaght's and the sheer visual luxury of Bristol's 19th-century almshouses symbolise the peculiar aesthetic generosity of the period. To us now it is both alien and a reproach: all wrong in theory, wholly right in practice. We have lapsed into the cities that Ruskin decried, "in which the streets are not the avenues for the passing and procession of a happy people, but the drains for the discharge of a tormented mob, in which the only object in reaching any spot is to be transferred to another." Victorian and Edwardian Bristol was a confused but sincere reaching after that Ruskinian ideal.

1. The Clifton Suspension Bridge, *designed by Isambard Kingdom Brunel; begun in 1836, completed in 1864*

The bridge is so obviously the world's symbol of Bristol that few people notice how unnecessary it was, and to an extent still is. Its road is of no importance and Clifton could well do without a link to the small, select suburb of Leigh Woods. When the span was first conceived around 1829 it was a case of 'let us bridge it because there is such a challenge in the gorge'. There was also an element of the picturesque in its conception as some of the rejected Romanesque and Gothic designs indicate. What was chosen was a fashionably Egyptian design and this, though the sphinxes were never added, accounts for the elegant batter of the great pylons. So it is in essence a Regency design. By 1851 the towers were standing but funds had run out and the ironwork was sold off to another Brunel bridge, the Royal Albert at Saltash. Brunel died in 1859. In 1862 work began again using the chains of Brunel's earlier Hungerford Bridge which was being dismantled and two years later the work was completed. The grandest and most successful landscape feature in the country, it is perhaps the only one truly to deserve that overused epithet 'sublime' because it does genuinely inspire terror and pleasure at one and the same time; hence its remarkable record of suicides.

2. Arno's Vale Cemetery Lodges, Bath Road, *1837–40 by Charles Underwood*

There is a wonderfully manic quality to Underwood's designs, nowhere more evident than in this pair that glower at each other like two stocky, but very authentic, monsters escaped from Paestum and now set by the A4 to guard the gates of respectable death. Death had, by the first decades of the century, become a profitable part of the capitalist system and Bristol was a relative latecomer to the process of setting up a limited company to run a burial place with style and a fair return for money. The wooded hillsides of the cemetery were once the parkland of Arno's Court and it is interesting that lodges should have been set up as if to some stately home, but obviously to indicate the class of tenant that was expected to occupy the graves. It was typical of Underwood's commitment to total authority that the lodge-keeper's bedrooms were lit by only the tiniest of windows cut into spaces of the frieze that would have been decorated, by a more genial architect, with metopes.

**3. Former Roman Catholic Pro-Cathedral, The Church of The Holy Apostles, now
disused, Park Place,** *begun in 1834 to designs by Henry Edmund Goodridge; later work of 1849 and
1870 by Charles Hansom*

For a great and relatively ancient city Bristol has had only moderate luck with its cathedrals. The
Anglican one on College Green is not on the major cathedral visiting circuit. This, the original
Roman Catholic example, is now a wonderfully atmospheric derelict, but a wreck for all that, and
its replacement in Clifton has yet to win hearts with its brutalist profile. Here on Park Place,
however, is Bristol's most Piranesian monument. Manifestly incomplete, the columns gain
imaginatively from the Corinthian capitals which they fail to deliver. The weeds flourish and the
row of lean-to buildings contrive to exaggerate the scale of what Goodridge planned by their
diminutive destitution.

4. Former Roman Catholic Pro-Cathedral

Hansom's narthex of 1870 is only another fragment of a rashly visionary project. This would have brought the stripey bacon of Siena to Bristol and crowned the hill with a five-storey tower topped by an octagon and finished by a spire. What Hansom was able to build is admirable and very Bristolian in being unrelated stylistically, not only to everything else in the city, but even to the beached whale of Goodridge's building that lies behind it. In its detail it is scholarly and the imaginative invention of the carving has been touched into something even more moving by the textures of decay. Unconsecrated now and forlorn, it is a place to savour.

5. St Mary on the Quay, *designed in 1839 for the Irvingite sect by Richard Shackleton Pope; converted into a Roman Catholic Church in 1843*

When the Irvingites commissioned R S Pope to build them a church in what was then still the harbour heart of the city, they allowed the Greek temple form to function as it was originally intended. The hexastyle portico draws the attention commandingly, even now when it is surrounded by much higher buildings, and being two bays deep yet windowless it combines a welcome of elegant style with the mystery of a hidden interior. The interior is not, of course, correctly windowless as the cella of a pagan temple would have been. It even has transepts. But St

6. Former Royal Western Hotel, now Brunel House, St George's Road, *1837–9 by Richard Shackleton Pope with the collaboration of Isambard Kingdom Brunel*

If, as has been claimed, Brunel sketched certain details of his proposed hotel and obliged Pope to incorporate them, this would explain the distinctly disjointed magnificence of the final elevation. Brunel must have wanted something that would evoke the flashy affluence of the Regents Park terraces to accommodate his putative trans-Atlantic passengers. As events turned out, Liverpool and Southampton stole the ocean liner trade and the hotel closed in 1855, since when it has staggered from hydro to offices to hotel and so to offices again. The façade is one that demands as much attention as admiration because so many features call for notice separately rather than as part of a unity. What isolates the two top storeys needlessly from the two lower ones is not the break from a flattened Corinthian order to crisp free-standing Ionic, but the complete change in the fenestration pattern. It is as if two men had designed two buildings and simply laid one upon the other. Enjoyable and indigestible as a heavy lunch, Brunel House suggests why Nash's original Buckingham Palace elevations were hastily covered up by Edward Blore. The Greek Revival seems to require a certain reticence.

Mary's is still curiously nonconformist in its impact. The façade is everything; austere side walls with blank niches hide all the body of the church and it is easy to understand why it was thought necessary to advertise the Christian function by a triumphalist inscription across the frieze. In such a disciplined building the detail is all important and close inspection reveals that Pope pressed his Corinthian to the limit. Almost naturalistic daisy flowers are cut into the capitals and whenever the chance to curve a flowing line occurs it has been exaggerated to give a florid grace to the initially feminine order. Indeed it is tempting to describe the portico as Composite rather than Corinthian. What gives a particular slenderness and height to the elevation is the exceptionally deep fluting of the columns which results in a multiple play of vertical shadows.

7. Temple Meads Station, *1839–41 by Isambard Kingdom Brunel and Richard Shackleton Pope; the company offices and booking hall of the original terminus on Temple Street*

There is little suggestion in this bland, symmetrical Tudor façade of the thrusting new age of steam. The choice of style, however, was almost certainly made by Brunel. Pope's Royal Western Hotel (**plate 6**), raised in 1837 to serve as a link between the railhead and ships to New York, was sumptuously classical. Perhaps Brunel wanted to suggest a safe, relaxed journey and chose this domestic note with that in mind. It is interesting to compare it with the Guildhall in Broad Street (**plate 15**) which Pope designed in 1843. Despite the difference in their functions the two buildings look interchangeable, but while the judges complained acidly about their law courts, this terminus building worked well. Out of that curious reverence which the GWR seems still able to inspire, the whole complex with the great train shed beyond has been allowed to survive and is now safely historic in an age of the heritage industry.

8. Temple Meads Station, *1865–78 by Sir Matthew Digby Wyatt; built when the lines were rationalised*

If one single epithet were needed to describe the general run of 19th-century architecture in Bristol it would have to be 'cheerful'. Here, as in so many buildings of the city, the mix of light red Pennant and creamy Bath stone tends to raise the spirits automatically despite the oddity of the design. The profile of the station entrance was originally even more bizarre as the fat central clock tower once carried a lively but incongruous Loire chateau-type spire. Most of the Wyatt family's Gothic output was unadventurously English Perpendicular so the station looks more of a piece now that the spire has gone. There can be few sites in Europe like this concourse at Temple Meads where old rivalries of warring railway companies are still evoked by their company offices in architectural battle, while Wyatt's absurd blond beast fronts the great curve of lines and sheds that put an end to the unnecessary conflict.

9. The Victoria Rooms, Queen's Road, Clifton, *designed in 1832 by Charles Dyer and begun in 1839*

This splendid building has always had a functional problem. Its authority is evident. It commands and gives character to an important road junction and merely to walk within its great Corinthian octostyle portico is to experience an exhilaration of the spirit. The quality of the carving is superb in depth and purity, the proportions of the columns swim with an almost mystic geometry. But what do you do in and with such a superb blind giant? For blind it is, and blindness is in the nature of the style. Both its return elevations have impressive hexastyle colonnades, but almost every window is in fact a niche of blank, smooth ashlar, an excuse for sharp masonry but not an entrance for light to the interior. It is a building made for night. Clifton built it as a set of assembly rooms for balls, concerts and lectures, but it misses that essential quality of cheerfulness and relaxation. Its golden, stony elegance is more spiritual than convivial, and so it has never flourished. One suspects that Bristol half intended the Rooms as a riposte to the rival port, Liverpool's St George's Hall, another Greek Revival giant in search of a function. But at least St George's Hall served for many years as law courts, blind Justice in a blind building. For a time the Victoria Rooms were animated by youth as the University's Student Union, but the students moved up the road to their modernist monster in the seventies. Now the great portico, proudly signed Charles Dyer Architect 1840, serves Bristol best as street scenery, bridging that curious urban gap between Clifton on the hill and the city on its winding waterway.

10. Clifton Vale, *1840–3 by Thomas Foster and William Ignatius Okely*

Okely, who had been Thomas Foster's apprentice, joined the two Foster brothers, Thomas and James, as a partner from 1827 until 1840 when this stair-terrace was begun. Bristol houses had always been inclined to assert their separate identity in a terrace by a vertical pilaster strip or 'lesene'. Here the bold downhill progression is marked by two lesenes, one set a foot or more below the other. The individual classical elevations are desperately plain, the door cut simply into shallow horizontal rustication beside an equally plain architrave. The architectural quality of the terrace depends upon the standardised balconies with the vestigial incline of their pediments whispering a Greek rhythm as they stride down towards the harbour. Mass production from a factory is beginning to offer the lower middle class an elegant address at cut-price rates.

11. Christ Church, Clifton, *begun by Charles Dyer in 1841, consecrated in 1844 and extended thereafter by John Norton, Ewan Christian and W Bassett Smith*

Nothing about this shrine of Evangelical Low Church Clifton is what it seems. What matters is to re-read John Betjeman's finest dramatic dialogue, 'Bristol and Clifton', which purports to take place actually inside Christ Church, and then to enjoy the paradox of these intensely Catholic

12. Tomb and Canopy of Raja Ram Mohun Roy, Arno's Vale Cemetery, *1844*

The Indian social reformer died suddenly when he was staying with Unitarian friends in Bristol in 1833. For ten years his body was buried in the garden of a house in Stapleton, but in 1844 it was moved to a plot in what was then unconsecrated ground in Arno's Vale Cemetery. This monument with its chatris and other appropriate south-Indian features was raised to his memory.

---

forms – soaring lancets, pinnacles and arrow-sharp spire – as the setting for archetypal Protestant worship. In Bristol's disunited urban landscape the spire of Christ Church is one of the rare picturesque dominants, while to Clifton itself it is the visual core, rising from the union of parkland and bourgeois housing as on the green of some infinitely superior village from which the peasants have been banished and where only gentry live. Dyer gave the inhabitants Christ Church to pray in and the Victoria Rooms to dance in and be merry. It is an odd commentary on times supposedly so secular that Christ Church still flourishes while the Victoria Rooms languish. As Dyer originally built it Christ Church was aisleless, but it had cruciform transepts so there was always that element of the near-cathedral about it which the tower and spire, completed by John Norton in 1849, confidently reassert. The trefoil-headed arcading of the tower is a subtle piece of scholarship to suggest that a tower of perhaps 1250 had been added to a nave and west front of 1220. Salisbury Cathedral is usually mentioned as a source but the cautious, even furtive, movement whereby the tower broaches into the spire owes more to the study of Northamptonshire churches like Kings Sutton of the 14th century. Thus, without ever breaking away from the slender purities of lancet forms, the church manages to imply a construction period of about 120 years.

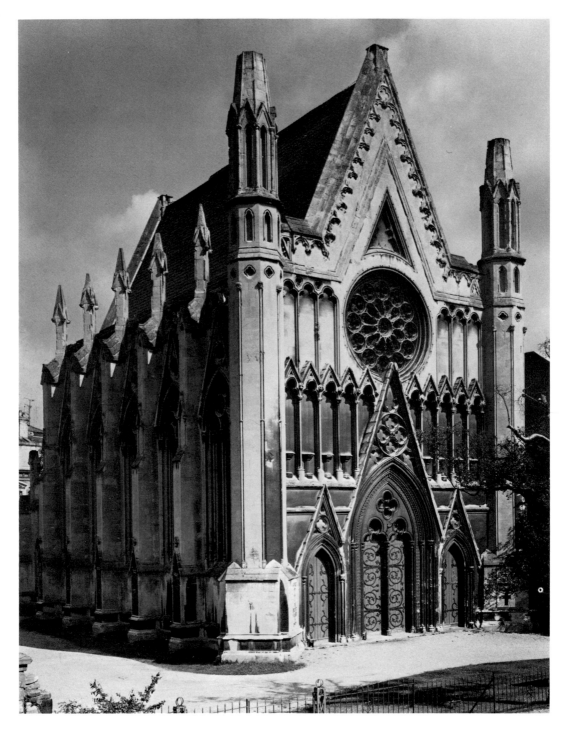

13. Buckingham Baptist Chapel, Queen's Road, Clifton, *designed by Richard Shackleton Pope in 1842 and completed in 1847*

The strident individuality and brash confidence of this building acts like a visual tonic among the bland terraces of inner Clifton. The Buckingham Chapel is essentially Regency Gothic, linear and two-dimensional, that has strayed into the wrong reign. After contriving a four-storey Greek Temple in the Royal Western Hotel (**plate 6**), Pope gave Bristol this Sainte Chapelle for the total immersion of the Baptists. More reliquary casket than chapel, its design concentrates the superficially-observed elements of a typical cathedral and compresses them into an enfilade of acute angles. Pope clearly had more feeling for a triangle than for an ogival arch and scorned

14. Queen Elizabeth's Hospital, Berkeley Place, *1843–7 by Thomas Foster*

Trapped in a rigid symmetry and designed as if to repel any entrance, this school building is a perfect illustration of the uneasy transition from Classical to Gothic in the English provinces. Building high on Brandon Hill, Foster could have achieved a fine composition in the picturesque castle style but what he designed cuts ruthlessly across its site evoking neither castle, abbey nor even college, only some giant and well-organised Dotheboys Hall. It is a tribute to the conservatism of Bristol institutions that it has remained unaltered and fully used to the end of the 20th century. Only the porter's lodge reveals a trace of that lightness and charm that were characteristics of Regency Gothic. In the main building there are no truly pointed arches and even five-centred Tudor arches are severely rationed. The central projecting feature, which it is impossible to describe as a tower, has an undeniable authority, but even there the trim of battlemented parapet is meagre because Bath stone came expensive and the prevailing dark red stone was quarried from the site. Thomas Foster, of the second architectural generation of his family, built enduringly but with an economy of talent and expense.

---

anything less than Lincoln in his quest for inspirational detail. Only the cheeky, grinning faces that top the buttress mouldings hint that he may not have taken his exercise too seriously. When first built the Chapel was much praised which is surprising. Its exact contemporary, the Highbury Congregational Chapel on Cotham Road, by William Butterfield, has the easy fenestration and aisled profile of a true village church, so scholarly Gothic was already abroad in Bristol. Another puzzle is that nonconformists in an area of conservative classical building should have adopted such 'Roman' forms. But the solution probably lies in the instant success of Christ Church, Clifton (**plate 11**). In its initial phase, as Charles Dyer built it in 1841, only a year before Pope designed the Buckingham Chapel, Christ Church was aisleless, towerless and acutely lanceolate: much closer to Pope's creation than now seems possible.

15. The Guildhall, Broad Street, *1843 by Richard Shackleton Pope*

As far as stylistic innovation goes this is Bristol's equivalent of Charles Barry's Palace of
Westminster, but there the comparison ends. It was the first Gothic Revival town hall to be built
in England and Pope, like Barry, had earned his reputation by designing classical buildings. This
shows in the rigid symmetry of the street façade, but the Perpendicular detail of the windows at
least is deeply carved and fairly committed. This cannot be said for the heads of the niches or the
disturbingly round-arched parapet of the central tower. Pope seems to have had his eye on the late
and unfinished Perpendicular detail of Cardinal Wolsey's building at Christ Church College,
Oxford, which may explain the abbreviation of the side pinnacles. As street furniture, and

16. Former Soap Works, now Gardiners Store and Warehouse, Old Bread Street

This is Bristol as it was in its industrial prime – a vast brick factory rising with a gawky self-confidence from a shapeless huddle of buildings dedicated to making money and to nothing else remotely pretentious. How long this original visual squalor will survive is anyone's guess. The new low, lean-to warehouse units are already marching in on the area, but it is to be hoped that Gardiners at least will survive. The machicolation over the firm rhythm of segmental-headed buttresses has a hint of Siena that is probably accidental and owes more to the turn of century industrial designs of the Frenchman Durand. It provides acres of solid floor space and may, therefore, last until a time when it can be viewed sentimentally.

---

particularly narrow street furniture, the Guildhall is effective. The side pinnacles and the central oriel overhang dramatically and, provided the eye keeps below the parapet, there is a general impression that here something solemn is going on appropriate to a large city of mediaeval origins. More can hardly be said. Bristol architects in the 19th century were a tight, exclusive body and there were times when the city would have benefited by bringing in an outsider for a major building. One judge described the interior as "the perfection of inconvenience" and a contemporary architect, Edward Godwin, described Pope as "that wretched mean fellow". The Guildhall, largely a complex of law courts inside, seems to express in this dark, overbearing street front the legal system as Dickens portrayed it in *Bleak House* rather than Justice in the abstract. Dickens was writing about a Regency rather than a Victorian England and this, by all appearances, is more a building of George IV than of Victoria.

17. Bank of England, Broad Street, *1844–6 by Charles Robert Cockerell*

For the most prestigious bank of all, Bristol brought in an outsider and a master of scale. The site was narrow and Broad Street is not broad. Dignity, order and security had all to be implied within these confines and the magnificent illusion begins with the twin porches. They project to the pavement as a first step in the process of giving a basically flat elevation a great complexity of depth and shadow. Also they are small yet appear substantial because of the exaggerated entasis of their neo-Egyptian styling. By contrast the Doric columns of the first two floors appear massive when they are actually no more than large. At the triglyph frieze level of the entablature, Cockerell

18. Tuscany House, Durdham Park, *circa 1850*

A house like this explains how the Italianate seduced Regency England away from neo-Classicism. At this early stage of the style, with a few correct columns, even the ghost of a pediment or two, it was such an easy step, and the move brought a relaxed diversity of asymmetrical parts where rooms could be extended to any shape. In addition there could be romantic balconies and that picturesque essential – a belvedere tower. A contemporary architectural pattern book by Francis Goodwin lists its advantages: from a tower room unwanted visitors could be spied on their approach and the butler forewarned, a gentleman could count deer from his snuggery or a lady could play a harp without offence to the household. This house has none of the fussy excess that gave the post-1860 Italianate of Pembroke Road and Tyndalls Park a bad name. It has smooth, expensive ashlar, not rough Pennant dug out from a quarry up the road, emphatic quoining, a shallow roof and the boldly projecting Tuscan eaves that gave it its name. Instead of the round-headed windows that lend an air of desperation to so many towers, the architect has set modified tripartite windows in the upper storeys to command views across the Downs. Both affluent and genteel, this is a villa for readings of Browning's 'Andrea del Sarto' and 'The Bishop Orders His Tomb'.

---

begins to play a subtle game of projected and recessed planes. The return walls of banded rustication have been marking a point of depth half-way between that of the porches and the colonnade, and now the frieze interrupts them with a confident, shadow-creating overhang. The severe ironwork with its anthemions gives the cornice the air of a balcony. Then behind the iron veil, melancholy and desperately sober with three levels of recession, come the three Roman arches. It is at this point that the tally of styles in a building of such apparent unity can be counted – Egyptian porches, Greek colonnade, Tudor mullions, Roman attic and a final Greek pediment. The art of the composition rests in the remarkable number of vertical and horizontal lines that lie behind the initial impression of grand simplicities.

19. Eastfield House, 40 Eastfield Road, Henleaze

In the first half of the 19th century this area of Bristol was farmland with just a scatter of merchants' villas within easy carriage reach of the city. Eastfield House was one of those, trapped now in suburbia. Even for Bristol, which is so rich in villas of the 1780–1850 period, this is outstanding in its absolute commitment to the Greek ideal by way of rectangles. Apart from the few, but decisive, touches of Attic decoration – anthemions, paterae, Ionic columns at the porch and an order in the first floor nearer to the Tower of the Winds than the true Corinthian – everything is rigidly straight to the point of being boxy. The house gives the impression of having been designed by a single-minded convert to the Greek ideal who was perhaps familiar with Cheltenham, where the Tower of the Winds order was used more often than in Bristol. All this points to Charles Underwood, the builder who went bankrupt in Cheltenham in 1821 but who re-established himself in Bristol, where the Arno's Vale Cemetery Lodges of 1837–40 (**plate 2**) were his earliest work and exhibit the same angular, almost fanatical purity as this remarkable house. Most of the restrained decoration can be found again on the return façades of his Worcester Terrace, Clifton of 1851–3 (**plate 20**).

20. Worcester Terrace, Clifton, *1851–3 by Charles Underwood*

Built in the second half of the Victorian century, Worcester Terrace is a monument to the stubborn rearguard action of neo-Classicism in Bristol. By its rectangularity and its passionate involvement with straight lines, it declares unmistakably the hand of Charles Underwood. The deep frieze with its paterae runs like a fusillade of full-stops above the tightly regimented Doric pilasters. Underwood must have enjoyed the austerity of the most primitive of the three great classical orders because his colonnade continues across the flanking recessed sections of the terrace and only stops when it comes to the two end pavilions. There is no danger of their verticals overwhelming the design because the architraves of the first floor windows stab emphatically across their lengths and the heavy horizontals of a continuous entablature provide another counter force. What is oddly weak in such a masculine performance is the ground floor. A terrace so ruthless and repetitive seems to demand a rusticated base, but Underwood has remembered his other preference – for uncluttered surfaces – and he has relied for support on the porches: Doric again but plain and stunted compared with the burden they appear to carry. As if in reaction against all this weary weight, Clifton's next terrace, Belgrave, is a riot of round-headed and Venetian windows.

21. St. Matthias College, Fishponds, *1851–2 by John Norton and Joseph Clarke*

This was originally built as the Gloucester and Bristol Diocesan Training Institution for School Mistresses. The Church of England was making a big effort at this time to counter the infiltration of nonconformists into junior education and a number of training colleges went up. Norton has consciously copied the open plan, the easy asymmetry of gables and the trefoil-headed windows from Samuel Daukes' slightly earlier College of St Paul in Cheltenham. As a result there is none of that unattractive rigidity and predictable sequence of pinnacles that spoils his churches. Buildings like this show how the adoption of Gothic is breaking up classical ideas of symmetry and preparing the way for the picturesque profiles and volumes of the Arts and Crafts, even though the actual detail looks infinitely distant.

22. Former Bristol and Exeter Railway Offices, Temple Meads, *1852 by Samuel Charles Fripp*

The gables and turrets of Fripp's Jacobethan design must have been intended as a public relations exercise: a defiant assertion of a threatened identity. It was obvious from the outset that the Bristol and Exeter and the GWR had common interests and that their lines should not end in two terminals a few hundred yards apart, but merge in one smooth profitable curve. Which was what happened in 1865. These offices were set at some psychic disadvantage in a depression on the concourse, and the two turrets that rise from the main block were probably intended as visual markers so that travellers would not be deflected by the Tudor offices of the GWR just across the yard.

23. Bristol General Hospital, Guinea Street, on the Bathurst Basin, *1852–7 by William Bruce Gingell*

Though much extended and mutilated by the loss of its curvaceous two-storey dome, Gingell's hospital demands attention as one of the few major buildings in this sea port to have been built with any intention of relating to and enjoying a position on the waterfront. There were "large and cheerful day rooms" in the tower for male and female convalescents where they could observe the comings and goings of passengers from the Welsh steamboats in the basin below them. The *Builder* remained highly suspicious: "The hospital occupies a peculiar, and, as it seems to us, ill chosen site … almost surrounded by water". A morbid dread of vapours had obliged Gingell to install a powerful ventilation system claimed to be capable of renewing the air of the entire building within minutes and hurling the tainted element upwards and out; "but we are not to be supposed to assent to the propriety of creating a hospital in such a situation as to render the elaborate system of artificial ventilation necessary". At that time, of course, the Floating Harbour was an open, and largely stagnant, sewer so the *Builder*'s correspondent had a case. This was Gingell's first commission in a city where he was to walk tall for almost 50 years. The fact that he was able to design a state of the art modern hospital with a steam lift, speaking tubes and nurses' quarters so sited that three nurses could overlook five wards, suggests how quickly he impressed the citizenry. His feat in placing three storeys of light, airy wards on a rockfaced podium of warehouses without incongruity, established him as a juggler in two styles and the master of two building types, one public and one industrial, both with rich pickings for an adaptable architect.

24. Victoria Square, South-West Side, *circa 1855 by John Yalland*

This least admired of the three terraces that define Victoria Square is a perfect demonstration of the dangers of Victorian eclecticism. J Marmont's earlier terrace, the neighbouring Royal Promenade, had, for all its display of round arches at ground and attic levels, held firm to basic classical reference and pulled the whole great battery of windows together by a strongly projecting central section and three-bay wings. In this south-western terrace with its much richer fenestration, the central feature should have been even bolder. Inexplicably, Yalland reduced it to three bays and the eye hardly registers it in the general profusion of detail. Round-arched forms are always prone to melancholy, like so many sad eyes raised heavenwards. They work best when, as in the Royal Promenade, they are seen to be supporting a heavy burden. But here the ground floor fenestration which should be the most massive is perversely the weakest and most underplayed, the next two storeys growing ever richer and heavier as they rise to the drama of the corbelled-out cornice. Then there is the matter of reference, a constant trouble in Bristol architecture of this period. Which century and which country are all these elevated cloisters intended to evoke? The answer must be Venice in its high 16th-century Renaissance. This is Clifton's riposte to St Mark's Square, but with no domes and no campanile to act as distractions from derivative and frankly uninspired motifs repeated 33 times in hot red stone.

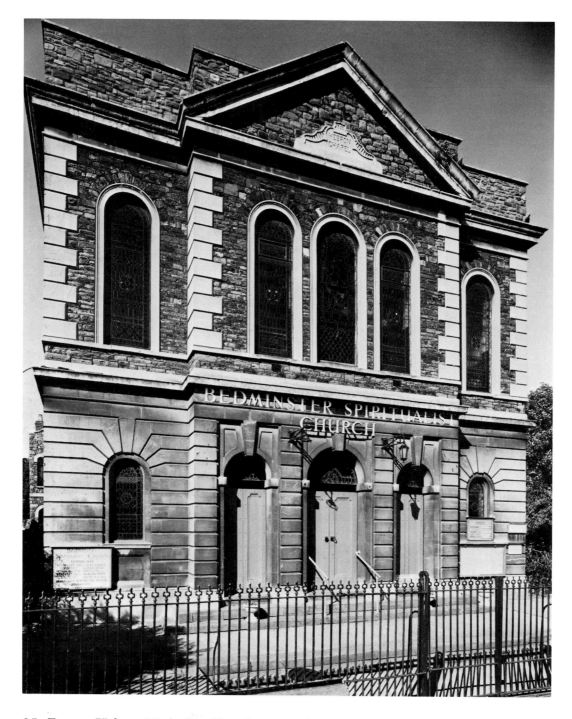

25. Former Hebron Methodist Chapel, now Bedminster Spiritualist Church, Hebron Road, Bedminster, *1853 by Henry Crisp*

Here is the essence of nonconformist industrial Bristol before the corruption of Gothic manners spread over from the established church. When Bedminster was a suburb of collieries and iron foundries, Methodism flourished in solid tabernacles like this with its base storey of classical ashlar and the melancholy grandeur of its round-arched windows set in rough Pennant stone. A local cathedral for the back streets of small, neat houses, its original congregation has deserted and it stands now in its large, weed-grown graveyard, the seat of a more exotic faith but of aspirations that John and Charles Wesley would have understood. Their father's rectory was, after all, desperately plagued for some years by poltergeist manifestations.

26. Arley Chapel, Cheltenham Road; formerly Congregational, now The Church of the Polish Catholic Community, *1855 by John Foster and Joseph Wood*

This chapel is one of several nonconformist ventures into the Rundbogenstil fashionable in the mid-century. It is only a short step from the earlier, immensely confident round arches of The Royal Promenade in Victoria Square. It stands like some cyclopean traffic marker, its semicircular narthex a geometrical symphony of curves – round arches, Tuscan windows with arched tracery, a rose with four circular insets and finally the belfry alive with the same arches and half-circles. Nonconformist communities were keen to rival the Gothic towered places of Anglican worship. They usually wished, however, to avoid the 'Romish' implication of the pointed arch and so the round arch was adopted instead. It is ironic that the building now seems completely appropriate to a Catholic community from Eastern Europe.

27. Royal West of England Academy, Queen's Road, *1857 by Charles Underwood and J H Hirst; ground floor addition of 1912 by S S Reay following a design by Henry Dare Bryan*

If a first reaction to this schizophrenic and exuberant façade is that Underwood could never have designed it, then the response is correct. He confined himself to the interiors, Hirst took the windows of the Barberini Palace in Rome, set them between Palladian niches and then topped the whole with a champagne confection of sculpture that automatically raises the spirits of the crowds passing to work on a Bristol morning. Reay's addition is repressive, authoritative and regrettable. It replaced an open staircase that was in keeping with the extrovert character of Hirst's composition. The date of this building and the partnership that raised it are significant. In 1857 an iron-hard neo-Classicist like Underwood had finally perceived which way the eclectic winds were blowing. If he could not bring himself to design in a more playful style at least he was prepared to take a fee working with someone younger and more adaptable who could and would. This is not

28. Former West of England and South Wales Bank, now Lloyd's, Corn Street, *1854–8 by William Bruce Gingell and T R Lysaght; sculpture by John Thomas*

This is a wonderful test piece to divide those who love architectural form and sculpture from those who merely like a quiet life and describe their condition as 'good taste'. To drag five whole bays of Sansovino's St Mark's Library from Venice and set them up in the relatively narrow confines of Corn Street was a tremendous expression of High Victorian self-confidence. At the same time, of course, it was an exact statement of the complete collapse of a native English, and certainly of a Bristol, tradition of design. When he built his Corn Exchange across the road a hundred years earlier, John Wood was borrowing from Palladio, another Venetian architect, but he modified and rearranged Palladio's motifs so extensively that the Corn Exchange was an original and distinctively English design. All that Gingell and Lysaght did when they prepared this bank was to give John Thomas the licence to carve even more richly and robustly than his Venetian precursors. When such reservations have been made the Bank is a superb piece of street furniture – grey Portland stone, golden Bath stone and deep shadow combine to give an effect of three-dimensional stage scenery. It may not belong but it certainly diverts and delights the unprejudiced pedestrian and it is the clearest proof of the influence of John Ruskin's *The Stones of Venice* on Bristol businessmen.

---

the picturesque Italianate but a relatively scholarly handling of 16th-century Roman prestige architecture. In the foreground can be seen the twining swags of Edwin Rickards' seaweed and his furtive octopus hiding under an improbably elegant rock (**plate 89**). It is a pity that Reay caught none of Rickards' playful invention.

29. No 16 Victoria Walk on Nugent Hill, Cotham

This north-east facing hillside below St Matthew's Church is one of Bristol's lost housing opportunities: a fine site developed in a desultory fashion with angular, vaguely classical villas and semis that rarely relate to each other and never come together to form a parish centre. No 16 Victoria Walk is an exception. The return façade on Nugent Hill shown here actually lights two houses not one, but it successfully pretends to be much grander than it is. Its stonework is a soft-textured grey Pennant that flatters the complex, shallowly-carved rustication and window panels with an impression of mellow antiquity. There is a sense of movement everywhere, basically in the comfortable bellied curve of the whole façade but also in the forward break of the two central windows which then break forward again on the ground floor. Although there is hardly a square foot of plain stonework, the detail is more Regency than Italianate and never seems fussy, only quietly rich. The wide eaves of the main house behind are Italianate and almost suggest that another architect was working there.

30. Colston Hall, Colston Street, *1864 by John Foster and Joseph Wood*

When Foster and Wood were commissioned to design what is still Bristol's largest and best-known concert hall, a curious thing happened. The architects obviously aimed at a grand statement of Italian Renaissance forms: an entertainment venue appropriate to the banks and business houses that were going up in and around Corn Street. But by sheer industrial infection from the 'Bristol Byzantine' warehouses that were the city's unique contribution to 19th-century architecture, they set their great overhanging cornice upon and surrounded the heavy authority of their arcade and loggia with a polychromatic dazzle of red and yellow brick, a material that in 1864 was mostly confined to the wharves and dockside. Most of the warehouses with their flat arches and colourful simplicity have been destroyed and now, quite inappropriately, the Colston Hall has survived to exemplify a style of which it was never a typical example. The detail of its cornice and string-courses is far too fine and correctly Italian to represent the average 'Byzantine' alternation of rough Pennant blocks in two colours. But there it stands. Its upper arcade, that once gave three-dimensional qualities to the massive top storey, has been blanked out with cement, and a canopy has been hung at precisely the right point to interrupt the rich rhythms of its entrance loggia. As a result, you hardly notice that the loggia is designed in the style of an Italy 200 years earlier than those Renaissance arches above it. Did Foster and Wood simply flip through pages of the *Builder* saying "I like that" and "Let's try this one"? All the fine interior fittings have been stripped away, but Colston Hall still functions for idiosyncratic Bristol, retaining, until this century at least, a style of its own based openly on industrial enterprise and doing things its own populist Bristol fashion with no strong national reference.

31 & 32. Clifton College, *begun in 1860 by Charles F Hansom and continued after his death by his partner Frederick Bligh Bond. Big School of 1862 is on the left, then Percival Buildings (1869), the Tower (1889) and the Chapel of 1868 but transformed by the octagon of 1907–10 by Sir Charles Nicholson*

Forever associated with Sir Henry Newbolt's nostalgic poetry, these are the archetypal fields of the late Victorian and Edwardian public school. The buildings around them deliberately and successfully create a stage scenery not only for learning but for patriotism. The boys may be in the middle of one of Clifton's duller sectors, next door in fact to the zoo, but the architecture excludes all that to evoke in the usual mix of cosy red Pennant and defining Bath stone a complex part-monastery, part-Tudor palace and even, after 1910, part-cathedral close. Big School has not the soaring proportions of Bristol Grammar School's gable ends and none of its jagged tension (**plate 55**) but the tower, much altered by Bond from Hansom's original designs, has a tremendous confidence. The star of David within a hexagon which Nicholson imposed on Hansom's rectangular chapel works excitingly and practically inside, but sits in some copper-green isolation on the exterior. Hansom's very High-Victorian, spiky belfry looks surprisingly comfortable considering it has no known mediaeval prototype. At its foot the war memorial exemplifies an image of the Christian knight and patriotic gentleman that would have been incomprehensible to the Middle Ages but that inspired thousands from schools like this to die in the trenches of Flanders.

33 & 34. Foster's Almshouses, Colston Street, *by John Foster and Joseph Wood: the range on the right with the oriel built first in 1861, the left-hand and central ranges, designed in 1872, built in 1880–3*

This is a Burgundian Gothic courtyard brimming with paradox. To spend so much money and imagination on housing the poor makes a point about the Victorians that is rarely noted. Why should it have been thought correct to build a Bristol almshouse in a style more closely associated with the wine sales of the Hotel Dieu at Beaune? The complex symmetry of the central range is riotously contradicted by the asymmetry of the flanking ranges, one of which came first in any case, so it is the centre that declared war. In another sense this is an intensely functional building. Not only do the circular stair turret and the galleries give a positively romantic access to flats which could so easily have been institutionalised like some Peabody building, but the whole prodigy of applied decoration – finials, ogee domes, arch over arch and cresting upon cresting – proclaim a wealth and cheerfulness that cannot have been without some benign psychic influence on its inhabitants. Perhaps the only reservation to be made about this positive haven is the sense of desperation in the quest for a style and the frantic expense made in search of a real city identity.

35. The Grand Hotel, Broad Street, *1864–9 by John Foster*

It will never be known what part the complex classical steeples of Christ Church and All Saints played in drawing the designs of the 19th-century commercial buildings ever upward in their elaboration to rival the skylines of the previous century. Certainly this photograph suggests that John Foster had more than half an eye on Christ Church when he crowned his new hotel in a superbly confident gesture with an open loggia and a tremendous overhanging cornice. Arguably the finest Victorian addition to the city, this building has what so few others in these central streets possess: areas of plain walling to rest the eye and allow the rhythm of the fenestration to take hold,

36. Former Bristol Lunatic Asylum, now Glenside Hospital, Stapleton, *1861–77*

Travellers driving out of Bristol on the M32 must often catch a glimpse of improbable towers and arched façades high up on their right like a West Country San Gimignano or the palace of some inland Doge. What they are seeing is yet another example of the Victorians' consistent high-mindedness in the treatment of the insane. Instead of hiding the unfortunate away in soulless blocks where administrative convenience and functionalism were the priorities, they built what are, quite literally, palaces of freely-interpreted Italianate motifs with not one, but several decorative towers and with formal water gardens and paths. The aim can only have been to raise the spirits of all who entered by creating a feeling of consequence, expense and care. The architect is unknown, but Samuel Whitfield Daukes, who designed Italianate terraces for Cheltenham and a vast Italianate Pauper Lunatic Asylum for Middlesex at Friern Barnet in 1849, certainly inspired the Bristol Asylum if he did not personally design it.

---

reducing by subtle degrees as it rises until the loggia breaks away from all native English expectations. Where R S Pope's hotel (**plate 6**) was ill at ease with four storeys, Foster makes six seem natural; one function of the great cornice was to conceal the attic. The projecting lower storey, originally occupied by shops, has been criticised by purists who look for a country palazzo when they should be enjoying a busy street scene. Between the main block and Christ Church, Foster, with perfect tact, set a much lower four-storey wing projecting boldly to phase into the scale of the church. The rich Corinthian pilasters of this wing were to have confused the wall surfaces of the whole hotel. John Foster must, at some stage, have rejected their verticality and allowed the concealed loggia to achieve the paradoxical effect of raising the eyes to an emphatically horizontal feature that locks the whole building comfortably into the line of the street.

37. Former Liverpool, London and Globe Insurance Building, 36 Corn Street, *1864 by William Bruce Gingell*

The Globe Insurance building is functional in that it proclaims success, but dysfunctional in that it also suggests prodigal waste of resources by a firm claiming to provide security and wise investment. A composite order supports a giant order of Corinthian rising through two storeys; this in turn supports an order of caryatids. All of these are doubled in deployment as they rise through no less than three ornately carved sequences of frieze and cornice to a double pediment. For once the description Baroque is justified as the coupled columns create a strong ripple of movement. Disappointingly, the caryatids are set too high up to make any street impact, but ferocious firemen with axes and three wild druid figures with long beards and moustaches animate

38. Channings Hotel, Pembroke Road, Clifton, *1865 by William Henry Hawtin*

This is the ultimate set piece of Bristol Byzantine in its domestic as opposed to its docklands mood; quite plainly it is not Byzantine at all but an indigenous suburban vernacular created from a fusion of Romanesque forms with French Renaissance ornament. Reputedly given by Queen Victoria to one of her ladies-in-waiting when she retired to get married, this is easily the finest house on Pembroke Road. The corner site has projected the architect into a tremendous jostle of movement and the usual bow windows have grown into something close to towers, defending the visual sight-lines from every angle of approach. This is real architecture, defying all categories, even those of symmetry and asymmetry. Hawtin should have been let loose from all those semis more often.

the portals on the ground floor. If the justification for all this expense is to carry the eye joyfully upwards then it succeeds. It will seem precious to find faults in such exhilarating freedom, but the rustication of the ground floor fails to imply strength because it is limited to alternate stones. More seriously the strong verticals of the Corinthian giant order are rudely broken by a horizontal bar between two floors which wilfully destroys the pattern of the rising rustication. Having said this, such savagery is quite within the spirit of the building. Director Mannerist, like the Artisan Mannerist two centuries before it, makes its own laws as it goes along.

39. The Elephant Inn, St Nicholas Street, *1867 by Henry Masters*

This is the very essence of 19th-century Bristol, a style that should be called Ruskinian Vernacular – wildly allusive, outrageously pretentious and an immediate pleasure to the eye. What is so intriguing is that the building on the right is handling Italianate mediaeval borrowings with absolute solemnity, while Masters plays irreverently next door with the slightly later forms of the Lombardic Renaissance. In the middle of it all the elephant looks down from a niche that is pure Rococo. This surely was a pub designed to attract the clerks and tellers accustomed to the architectural standards of Gingell's West of England and South Wales Bank (**plate 28**). The Elephant is perfect tavern architecture: a narrow street front that seizes the eye in the face of strong competition, then suggests at one and the same time both privacy and riot. Its neighbour, however, seems from those narrow Gothic arches to cry out for mortification and prayer. Sadly, Henry Masters appears to have ended his career as a sanitary engineer. On the strength of The Elephant he deserved better.

40. Premises on the North-East Side of Victoria Street

This is the texture, the human scale and the rich stylistic diversity that Bristol has lost or is losing from so many of its main streets. The first two buildings on the left both deploy a giant order of Ruskinian Gothic. They are ordinary commercial premises but in their separate, highly individual ways they reach for the aesthetic pretentions of a Venetian palazzo because their age rated trade as a noble activity rather than as mere cut-price warfare. Next comes Platnauer Brothers with wild Corinthian pilasters and incised anthemions. The round-arched classical building by its side is a possible survivor of what stood here before Victoria Street was cut through to Temple Meads Station from Bristol Bridge. Last in the row was once a public house in extrovert Italianate. Its pilasters and string-course are all formed of anthemion-patterned terracotta tiles and its two windows both indulge themselves in the ornate forms of the Lombardic Renaissance. When the average developer looks at such a row he sees the cost of the repair of all this detail and workmanship, the diversity of the floor levels and the expense of a conversion into a single block of connected offices. Then, after a little mental arithmetic and unless the community's leaders are both alert and sensitive, the bulldozers come in and another building like the aptly named General Accident block across the road goes up on the site. In this way a city loses its individuality and its citizens become accustomed to visual malnutrition.

41. The Granary, Welsh Back, *1869 by Archibald Ponton and William Venn Gough*

That most overused of descriptive terms, 'unique', should be reserved by law for buildings of The Granary's brilliant strangeness. And why was John Ruskin never brought here to record his admiration for a building which, more than any other in Britain, expressed his architectural ideals using the forms of the mediaeval city states of Italy to bring function and grace to the satanic mills of industry? Its patterning and decorative interpenetration of forms are extraordinarily inventive and disturbing. All the great height weighs down on its lowest row of delicate ogee points above the ground floor arches and the solidity of its angles rests on the gallant frailty of polished granite columns in undercut niches. The battlements bristle with the forked merlons of Tuscany and all in between are row upon row of openings various in shape though logical in their implied strength.

42. Former Bristol Library and Philosophical Institution, Queen's Road, now University Refectory, *1867 by John Foster and Archibald Ponton*

Foster is usually credited with the elevations of this distinguished building and Ponton with the plans. But despite the existence of Foster's engaging watercolour, which shows the building as it was intended to look, it is hard to believe that the concept and the main outlines were not Ponton's. John Foster's designs were sound but Ponton, with buildings like the Avon Insurance in Broad Street (**plate 43**) and The Granary on Welsh Back (**plate 41**) was the real convert to Ruskinian ideas and could give that extra quality of imagination and commitment to what he built. A building of this quality, sited so strategically, deserved a sensitive and costly renovation; instead it has been virtually stripped of charm and colour. Only its fine bones and profile survive. It has lost the delicately spired shrines that lightened its angles. Its niches never received their intended statues, the cornice was never carved with leaf patterns and the Gothic parapet has gone. The two balconies of Foster's watercolour were not built and the colour contrast of its stone has dimmed. Lastly, and most recently, the essential open character of its loggia has been shattered by a glazing scheme. Some day the city and the university must notice the treasure in their midst and set about restoring it to its former magnificence.

Originally they were unglazed and the decorative mesh of brickwork within them not only allowed fresh air to penetrate, but the eye to take the impression of the wall's vast depth. All accounts of this triumph of Bristol's dockside dwell on the ingenuity of the great lifts concealed within its angles, and on the lucid engineering which conveyed sacks of grain down from its towering 100 feet of ten floors to slide through the decorative roundels of the podium into waiting carts. But were The Granary's best days perhaps those later ones when it was a famed venue for Heavy Metal bands, and the thunder of violent music delighted leather-clad youth in their packed hundreds? For surely a great and beautiful building inspired by the feudal palaces of Siena was made for music, revelry and enjoyment and not for inanimate loads of corn? Restored now with consummate taste, its red Cattybrook bricks chequered with black and buff, and its relieving sections of Bath stone scraped, The Granary will house offices and only become vital again at Christmas time.

43. Avon Insurance Building, Broad Street, *1868 by Archibald Ponton*

A dazzling clarity of light and lens combine here with a virtuosity of mason's work. The merit of such mid-century stonework has been given the restoration it deserved. Each separate block of stone was individually tooled to create textures that are only subliminally absorbed at pavement level. The colour and the grain of the rock have been applied into patterns of contrast with an artist's awareness, and shadow invited to dramatise reflected light. There is even humour in the posture of the wriggling gryphons and cramped lions. This then is Ruskinian theory put into practice: the forms of the Middle Ages revived to frame a business house for a 19th-century city, the masons allowed, within reason, to express their own individuality in the stone they carved. But

44. Alpenfels, North Road, Leigh Woods

The Gorge at this point acts as a stylistic *cordon sanitaire* shielding the polite suburb of Leigh Woods from the usual Bristol influences and restrictions. Walking its quiet roads it is possible to believe that you are in Surrey, the gardens large and leafy, more than a little brick architecture and a general escape from the rather tight, stony formalism of the city's middle-class housing of the 19th century. All this is post-1865 when the Suspension Bridge was opened and even Clifton moved slightly down-market as the seriously rich fled to the green woods. Alpenfels is of a piece with this exclusive apartness yet not quite as detached as its neighbours. It looks back across the Gorge to Clifton and there was an earlier villa on the site before the bridge was built. The beautifully-jointed local limestone subtly undercuts the alien cuckoo-clock styling, allowing the house to seem more at home than it should be. Nothing in the detailing has been stinted: the lacey fall of the bargeboards, the triple projection of the corbels that project rather than support the eaves and balconies that could well contain the chorus in at least a modest staging of 'Tannhauser'. The Bristol bourgeoisie was beginning to think international when this was built.

---

does it work? Is it functional? And the answers have to be both 'yes' and 'no'. Yes in the sense that it pleases the eye and disturbs the imagination. No in the sense that it is an effective way of darkening the internal rooms by setting up a double curtain of walls. Historically it is suspect as it combines clerestory windows that would be at home in Notre Dame, Paris with those dubious 'Caernarvon' arches that were such a cop-out for Victorians when a rectangular form was needed as they are very rare in authentic mediaeval architecture. In the next year, 1869, Ponton, aided by William Venn Gough who had yet to become a full partner in the firm, would begin his masterpiece – The Granary on Welsh Back (**plate 41**). In this present building his confidence, scholarship and feeling for definition can be sensed like a coiled spring waiting to unfurl.

45. Westbury-on-Trym Village Hall, Waters Lane, *1868–9 by John Foster and Joseph Wood*

The patron, Henry St Vincent Ames of Cote House, was one of those benign Victorian squires who would, out of his own pocket, provide a superior social centre for the community he lived in and at the same time consider sacking the new caretaker because his 40-year-old wife had become pregnant. "It is a great nuisance certainly" his diary records. While the boldly-outlined hexagon of the hall may owe a little to the Gothic vivacity of Cote House itself, Foster and Wood seem to have had their eyes most firmly on cathedral chapter houses, a remarkably ambitious source for such a relatively humble building. Mr Ames was devoted to choral work and probably directed the design along lines that would have seemed appropriate to the performance of religious cantatas. The Pennant stone of which the hall and the keeper's house are constructed is of an unusual orange colour which does much to lighten the impact of a very seriously conceived design.

46. Synagogue, Park Row, *1871 by Henry Crisp*

This portico has a power and exotic presence out of all proportion to its size. The actual synagogue behind is invisible, as the church is invisible behind the columns of St Mary on the Quay (**plate 5**). All we are given is darkness behind a simple arch of triumph so that the eye is caught up by the Hebrew inscription, inscrutable to the uninitiated, but automatically suggesting the dreadful warning in John Martin's painting of Belshazzar's Feast: "Thou has been weighed in the balance and found wanting". Beneath runes like these, even Crisp's three-light window appears inscrutable. The arch was probably re-used from another building.

47. Bristol Cathedral, *the nave and western towers designed in 1867 by George Edmund Street and completed with considerable alterations by John Loughborough Pearson after Street's death in 1881*

When he designed a nave and western towers for Bristol cathedral in 1867, Street must either have suffered a most uncharacteristic loss of nerve or been pressured into a solution that would accommodate a large congregation with concert hall openness. Instead of rebuilding and extending a heavy, dark Norman nave as prelude to the brilliant spatial devices of Abbot Knowles'

48. Greenbank Cemetery Chapels, Eastville, *circa 1870*

There was something suggestive of the atmosphere of a Joe Orton black comedy in the outcry that arose when Bristol City Council proposed to demolish these chapels in 1990. The local vicar reported that his telephone rarely stopped ringing as local people expressed their anger. Tea rooms, a health club, a library and a social club were among the ideas put forward for their re-use. One clergyman plaintively urged that one of the two structures might make a good chapel. What was interesting in all this was the revelation of a popular aesthetic appreciation poles apart from the bland elevations that have been foisted on the public over so many years in the name of good design but in the actual interests of economy. The chapels have great visual character of an eccentric kind. The activity of their apsidal endings, the battery of sharp gables and the doleful self-mockery of the central bell turret may not be beautiful in any obvious sense, but they combine to a memorable whole and give an appropriate melancholy consequence to death. William Wood Bethel handled the east end of his St Agnes, Newfoundland Road in a manner reminiscent of this hyperactive pair.

14th-century choir, Street resorted to a competitive response. His nave is a mere scholarly anticipation of all the technical innovations in the choir vaults. As a result, all vistas are open up to the high altar; there is no drama of contrast, no mystery of darkness before light. Pearson's handling of the western towers after Street's death in 1881 was a further misfortune. The intended spires, being only blunt, lead-covered pyramids, were no loss. What impoverished the west front was the cutting down of the buttresses. Street had designed them to rise up to the final parapet. This would have pulled all three stages of the towers together and given an impression of diminishing breadth. He also proposed to give depth to the central rose window by setting a pinnacled stair-turret to project generously from the inside western corners of each tower. Inexplicably Pearson built these on the outside eastern corners of the towers where they have minimal impact. The angels above the west door crown and cense an empty niche, an interesting reminder of low church prejudices which ran strongly in this diocese during the 1880s.

49. Former Lodge to Cote House, now St Monica's Lodge, Durdham Down, *1874*

Some dreadful composite term such as 'Jacoredland' or 'Redlandobethan' would have to be devised adequately to categorise the vast acreage of warm red stone and indeterminate styles in north-west Bristol. But here, isolated on the Downs and with woods behind, the eye can absorb the unpretentious charm and freedom of the mid-Victorian domestic. In all this modest little building the architect has only repeated himself once, with the two ground floor windows. Everywhere else there is invention: a porch worthy of a chateau on the Loire with the profusion of François Premier, a tower that turns out to be an apsidal wing, eaves broken by a jaunty architrave and a generous bow window to spy out the approach of carriages along the drive. As so often in this study the wealth and aesthetic confidence of the age forcefully comes over. The patron was Henry St Vincent Ames who had recently paid for the building of Westbury Village Hall (**plate 45**). Did he use the ever pliant architectural partnership of Foster and Wood again for this new lodge to his Cote estate?

50. Avoncourt, North Road, Leigh Woods, *circa 1875*

Tudor detail on villas of this size very often tempted the architect to a cowardly symmetry. Sharply-pointed arches (it is impossible to describe them as 'Early English') on such a house are always more visually exciting. They tend to throw the proportions upward in an agonised heightening – a perpetual stony prayer to heaven – and the pronounced asymmetry at least would have pleased Pugin, though he would not have approved the round bay. Ruskin might have had a good word for the crisp, lively floral carving around the porch. If the erratic path of the flat string-course is followed it would seem that the bay window was an afterthought, a typical Bristol feature added to capture light from more than one point of the compass and highly functional for all its oddity. Houses such as this were being built in the city in the early 1870s and Avoncourt is probably one of the first in Leigh Woods after the opening of the Suspension Bridge. The suburb later assumed a more relaxed building style. George and Henry Godwin, architects of the spiky Clifton Drinking Fountain (**plate 51**) are the most likely designers for this uncompromising house.

51. Drinking Fountain, Bridge Valley Road, *1872 by George & Henry Godwin*

Pure water still gushes freely at the touch of a brass button from this Gothic triangularity. It is made of Box limestone with red Mansfield stone for contrast in the voussoirs. The columns are of Rouge Royal marble and the steps that make you climb as to an altar to quench your thirst are of humble Pennant. Alderman Proctor, late High Sheriff and a Merchant Venturer, presented it to the citizens. Bristol Waterworks promised to supply the liquid at a cost of one shilling per metred thousand gallons and the experience of using it is a miniature time trip in itself.

52. Main Gate Lodge, Ashton Court, Leigh Woods, *1877 by John Foster and Joseph Wood*

Ashton Court has an outstanding set of park gate lodges, all dating from the 19th century and increasing in size and the convenience of their accommodation as the century advanced and social attitudes to servants altered. This is the latest and most generously designed of them all. Two substantial houses for park keepers are linked in an exactly symmetrical composition which is then given the single unbalancing asymmetry of the high turret on the right. From this a watch could be kept on a whole sweep of the drive and the road leading to the suspension bridge so that the gates could be opened for carriages of the Smyths and their guests. Foster and Wood designed here in their well-tried Grammar School style (**plate 55**) with the bold massing and heavy detail suitable to Pennant stone and Bath dressings. They were working at the Court for Sir Greville Smyth who clearly intended his home to loom on the Bristol social horizon as a local version of Windsor Castle. John Foster may even have had Sir Jeffry Wyatville's heavy alterations to Windsor in mind.

53. Nos 9-11 St Stephen's Street, now The Exchange Wine Bar, *1875 by J H Hirst*

This is a perfect building for a debate on architectural morality which must, however, end in the conclusion that most judgements are subjective. In one sense Hirst's elevation is outrageous, an affront to the average English sensibility that expects buildings to rise by a firm sequence of stages, the storeys growing lighter as they climb in a modest progression. It is also derivative and unscholarly, quite an ingenious paradox. None of the capitals in the upper storey manage to break through to the cornice for the obvious reason that Hirst could see no way of getting them through the pendulous ranks of brackets without a nasty visual accident. One capital has even lost its

54. Bengough's Almshouses, Horfield Road, *1878 by John Foster and Joseph Wood*

Something interesting was going on when Foster and Wood designed these 19th-century almshouses immediately next to Colston's Almshouses of 1691 on St Michael's Hill. They had evidently realised that the charm of Colston's arose from its fumbling and incorrect handling of classical detail. So they went back even further, perhaps about 50 years, and attempted to reproduce work of that period now known as Artisan Mannerist (c 1630–6) when masons trained in Jacobean work were trying to absorb classical devices. Hence Foster and Wood's amusing, correctly 'incorrect', central feature where a door with a broken pediment sits within two or even three higher pediments, all deliberately clumsy in their arc or angles. What the partners appear to have been reaching towards was the Arts and Crafts style that was to become current only late in the next decade with its relaxed play of homely vernacular effects. If that was their intention they failed for two reasons. The first was that they got the scale wrong: the storeys are too high and the building as a result sits uncomfortably on its sloping site. The second is the harsh texture of the machine-made bricks which more than a century has failed to soften. Successful Arts and Crafts work at the turn of the century would depend very largely on the quality of its materials: hand-made bricks, wrought ironwork, the texture of stone. Here at Bengough's the architects were still trapped in the technical breakthrough of the industrial revolution; as a result they have produced a mere institution when a cosy haven was almost within their grasp.

---

supporting pilaster and hangs irrelevantly between two windows which, had they been just a little smaller, could easily have let a pilaster through. On the credit side, derived from the Venetian palazzos of Michiel and Vendramin-Calergi as it may be, there is no other building in Europe remotely like it. Everything about the elevation is disturbing and demanding. It bludgeons the narrow street into cowed visual submission. Though the arcade stands on stilts, legging itself across two storeys, it is too weak to carry two jutting cornices with huge Tuscan windows between them and a pediment with balustrade above. Someone must have told Hirst to make a statement that could not be ignored. He did exactly that and if the result is ill-mannered then it has bad company and it still remains memorable.

55. Bristol Grammar School, University Road, *1875–9 by John Foster and Joseph Wood*

It must sometimes seem that the whole of 19th-century Bristol, or at least all its significant buildings, owed their design to the firm of Foster and Wood. They must indeed have been very well connected, but the sheer scale and easy relaxed Perpendicular detail of a hall like this goes some way to explain their omnipresence and also the complete absence from Bristol of any work by Sir George Gilbert Scott. With Foster and Wood to hand, the city had no need of a Scott. The functional practicality of what they built to house the Grammar School on the last of its several house removals is proven by the fact that the great hall still easily contains its morning assemblies and the nine classrooms included in the package are still loud with children. Scale and colour-

56. Royal Hospital for Sick Children, St Michael's Hill, *1883–5 by Robert Curwen*

This building makes a potent case for *architecture parlante*. Gothic Revival forms have a great reserve of drama. They can, as in the Palace of Westminster, raise the spirits by towers soaring like a heavenly city up from an ordered base. Or they can, like Manchester Town Hall, leave a tax-payer confused, impressed and exhilarated. They should also, by their flexibility of form, their curvaceous arches and the freedom of their carved figures, be able to offer a sick child a scale and an interest that will be comforting. To enter a children's hospital could be like entering a benign Disneyland of fairy turrets and peeping elves. Curwen has made even less of the Gothic in 1883 than R S Pope made of the Guildhall in 1843 (**plate 15**). Trapped in symmetry and emphasising that trap by the Bath stone heightening of his architectural incidents, he has produced an elevation that speaks no other word than the plain 'Institution'. More disturbingly, the large 20th-century extension to the hospital fails even to say that. With the Maternity Hospital across the road and the University Library at the corner of Tyndall Avenue, it is as if a coven of witches had conspired to blight the most beautiful street in Bristol just as it crested its steep ascent.

---

contrast are what carry the building. Its outline is subordinate to the warmth of its pink Pennant stone and the bold clash of the Bath limestone that flickers nervously up and down each buttress and dramatises the frantic jig of its crow-stepped gables. The Pennant emphasises stability and repetitive routine, the limestone saves the huge, scholarly ark from tedium and visual complacency. Finally, the extreme attenuation of its rocketting clock-tower gives the necessary vertical emphasis at an unexpected point of focus. Crowning it all is the Heath Robinson canopy raised absurdly high on its ironwork supports like some engaging metalwork master's eccentricity: the first landmark, in fact, of the city to anyone approaching from the north over the Downs. This time Foster and Wood may reasonably have congratulated themselves.

57. Former City Fire Office, Clare Street, *1889 by E Henry Edwards*

Cut off the bottom storey and you have a reasonably handsome office building, a self-indulgent compression of motifs from mid 17th-century English vernacular. What, for instance, are all those Ipswich windows doing between coupled Ionic pilasters? But it is all well lit and prosperous looking and Edwards has thought up a real Arts and Crafts innovation with the deep eaves gallery that raises the helmet of the roof so gallantly. Never mind its lack of function and the darkness of those windows; it gives depth and character to the composition. It would, however, be interesting

58. Stoke Bishop Hall, Stoke Hill, *1885 and perhaps by Edward Gabriel*

Nothing could present a more complete contrast in spirit than the 'village' halls of the two neighbouring Bristol suburbs, Westbury-on-Trym (**plate 45**) and Stoke Bishop. Here, although the rough and ruddy Pennant has been used for the main walls, not only has a more cheerful hue of rock been chosen, but almost all the upper surfaces are tile-hung and suggest Surrey far more than Gloucestershire. The white-painted woodwork, the plaster pargetting and the touches of mid 17th-century vernacular in the fenestration all prove that Gabriel, if he was in fact the designer, was an enthusiastic follower of Richard Norman Shaw. While the hall captures the mock-bucolic atmosphere of Stoke Bishop perfectly and is in itself an attractive centrepiece to the suburb, it occasions some regret as it signals firmly the end of a local and distinct tradition of design.

---

to know why that shaped gable was slipped in at the end. Was it for more direct sunlight? The ground floor is a disaster. There is too much plain surface to support all that activity above and the arches rest on squidgy little pilasters that, when their turn comes, have only a thin window sill for support. Why use classical details only to make fun of them (the same could be said about recent Post-Modernism)? No self-respecting business building wants to be a joke. Finally, the main entrance is weak, its cornice supports nothing and the double oriel above it is left looking pot-bellied. All that accepted, it remains a building that engages and then puzzles the eye.

59. Former Port of Bristol Authority, now Queen Square House, Queen Square, *1885 by William Venn Gough*

Gough's Port of Bristol building demands a delicate appraisal. It ignores the style and the rooflines of its Georgian neighbours and perhaps it was tactless to clean and restore its original vivid colour scheme quite so thoroughly. Nevertheless in a large square of unassuming buildings it does provide a vigorous focal point, albeit on no particular logical axis of attention. Venn Gough was never dull and here, unlike his Colston's Girls' School (**plate 60**), he has confined himself to one distinct

60. Colston's Girls' School, Cheltenham Road, *1891 by William Venn Gough*

This overwhelming essay on the theme of streaky bacon needs to be considered in the context of the street which Gough set out to savage. Cheltenham Road is, at this point, dull and whatever else Colston's Girls' School can be accused of it is never tedious. Its architect had become Archibald Ponton's partner while Ponton was completing The Granary on Welsh Back (**plate 41**) and that brilliantly successful polychromatic design seems permanently to have infected Gough with the need to outpoint it in confrontational challenge. Here, unlike his Port of Bristol Authority Building in Queen Square (**plate 59**), the school does no environmental damage and probably makes several hundred passers-by feel aesthetically superior each day. The great thing about such architecture is that the asymmetry of its wings, the clash of Cattybrook brick with buff terracotta and the impenetrable confusion of historical reference all demand a response. Even if they provoke distaste in sensitive souls, these façades have had an educational value; to dislike a building is to learn what you like. Monotony and indifference are the true evils. This stew of motifs from the Renaissance of all those countries like England, Flanders and Germany that took stylistic indigestion from their first taste of Italy, must be a tremendous joke to the pupils who learn good taste and judgement inside its walls. Was Venn Gough instructing or consciously diverting?

---

style. His façade has a rich unity and its echoes of Antwerp when that city was at the height of its early 17th-century prosperity were, at the time, suitable for another great port. What the elevation desperately needs are a few areas of inactive brick and terracotta for the eye to rest so that the frenzied articulation of columns that support buttresses which end up merely supporting small urns, can be disentangled and absorbed. Perhaps Venn Gough was anxious that such, ultimately critical, analysis should never take place and he may also have wished to distract attention from the building's basic asymmetry.

61. Former Convent of the Sisters of Charity, now St Agnes Retreat House, Redcatch Road, Knowle, *1890–1, designed by John Dando Sedding and completed after his death by assistant Henry Wilson*

A building like this in the early Arts and Crafts style depends heavily on the quality of its materials and the workmanship involved. All that costs money, and when the Sisters of Charity were constructing this combined community house and orphanage, which they styled in the fashion of the day an 'Industrial School', cash was short and corners had to be cut. This shows. Much of the stone carving that Sedding had designed for the mediaeval-style gate tower was never added: statues had been intended for the niches on each side and above the door. More seriously, the timber work, so basic to convey the organic growth of a real 15th-century manor house, is thin and

62. Former John Lysaght Ltd, St Vincent's Works, now Blagden Packaging, Silverthorne Lane, St Philip's Marsh, *1891–3 by R Milverton Drake*

Here, perhaps more than anywhere else in the city, is evidence that 19th-century merchants really were 'princely' in their vision and planning and that the term is not mere hyperbole. The continuity of round-arched design on Lysaght's site along Silverthorne Lane is striking. John Lysaght, a Bristol-educated Irishman, was given the original galvanising plant of only seven workers in 1857, but he soon expanded it to include earlier foundry buildings in a primitive Rundbogenstil and even two neo-Norman gate lodges. The later office block was devised by Milverton Drake with wages, timekeepers, muniments, stationers, country and roofing departments all arranged around the literally glittering octagon alight with Royal Doulton tiles (**plate 63**). Quite what image Milverton Drake was attempting on the exterior it is hard to say. Free-form Norman might serve as a description but 'Ruritanian Romanesque' catches its self-inflated grandiosity perfectly. Inside (**plate 64**), there is a central mosaic floor emblazoned with Bristol's city arms. Italian grotesque work enriches the spandrels of the arches and snarling metal heads of panthers lend an odd ferocity to the railings of the gallery. Below the tiled and glazed dome a painted frieze of golden ships from an Egyptian galley to a Bristol-built steam warship reminds the visitor that Lysaght's did have maritime interests in addition to its most profitable trade in corrugated iron sheets to the Australian outback.

---

the studding has an applied look. There is an artful blend of coursed rubble and ashlar over the gate to give a sense of age and repair, also the usual Arts and Crafts mix of render, tile-hanging and timber-framing, but Bristol workmen seem to have baulked at the pargetting that Sedding had proposed. Wilson simplified the fenestration of the end wing, cut out a double oriel of Sedding's favoured Ipswich windows and added a long ski-slope of roofing. The result is suburban though relaxed and non-institutional. Sedding had spent eight years in Bristol between 1868 and 1875, but seems not to have absorbed the local vernacular of hinterland villages like Pucklechurch; he still turned for his models to the eastern counties.

63. Former John Lysaght Ltd – interior

64. Former John Lysaght Ltd – interior

65. E Shed, St Augustine's Parade, *1894 by Edward Gabriel*

Gabriel has transformed the essentially relaxed and suburban motifs of the Arts and Crafts into something more formidable and appropriate to dockland by the grids of stone that he has applied across the brickwork. The urns around the base of the dome and the ironwork on top of the gate piers show that this was a no-expense-spared job, and Gabriel's building still gives an admirable focal point to that peculiar corner where College Green dips down into the Centre. Architectural motifs can be as infectious as a cold and in this area there are at least six other domes or semi-domes, some of them very recent, that have 'caught' Gabriel's dominant feature, which, of course, he had himself borrowed.

66. Former Bracken Hill House, now University Botanic Gardens House, North Road, Leigh Woods, *1895 by Henry Shaw*

This casually affluent-looking house is an interesting example of how architectural fashions, in this case Norman Shaw's handling of the Arts and Crafts to produce cottage-mansions, were disseminated. Henry Shaw was a Londoner and here he has brought Surrey to Bristol with risqué pargetting of mermaids, terracotta finials, an ogee dome and much tile-hanging. Because Arts and Crafts designs were invariably based on small vernacular cottages and farmhouses, they rarely compose well when inflated to produce a large family house. Here the plan lacks coherence, suggesting none of the subtleties of Lutyens's organic profiles. But this flaw is more than excused by the vitality of the surface decoration, in particular a menacing terracotta beast that crouches on the gable end of the garden entrance porch.

67. Belvedere, North Road, Leigh Woods

There is something so direct and logical about this house that it is hard to see why there are not hundreds more designed with the same single-mindedness. If you have a house that almost commands a splendid view, as here the woods of Nightingale Valley and the Avon Gorge, why not set up a true belvedere on the roof with a gallery all around it to make up the extra few feet in height that will make all the difference? When the English climate makes the gallery impossible for half the year there are ample rooms behind for a sheltered but still panoramic retreat. Belvedere is very typical of the faintly eccentric apartness of Leigh Woods from the rest of the city.

68. Nos 40 & 42 Downleaze, Sneyd Park, *1898 by Henry Dare Bryan*

By the end of the century middle-class housing was in a golden age of invention and diverse charm. This is not one house but a pair, the semi-detached posing convincingly as a small manor house of some uncertain period and of several counties. The tile-hanging is of Surrey, that home county most dear to the Arts and Crafts movement, but the grey stonework is of the Bristol hinterland. Ipswich windows from East Anglia are bowed out to catch the suburban sun and the stocky Doric columns of the porch and the overhang are Artisan Mannerist of the same 17th century. The flowing cartouches of stone beneath the first floor windows suggest the heraldry of gentry status to flatter the aspirations of the bank managers and solicitors who would have been the natural occupants. Everywhere there are the textures and whimsical, delicate touches of 'sweetness and light': egg-and-dart running along the string-course, little capitals and fading pilasters on the mullions of the lower windows. If the house on the left has gained a bow window by hiding its porch, around the corner you can be sure that the right-hand house contrives a bow where the other conceals its porch. This means that the individual room plan of each semi will be quite different to that of its neighbour. Consider, for instance, how the tall Tudor stack on the right will alter the layout of the attic bedrooms. Richard Norman Shaw's influence has come to polite Bristol and with more luck and confidence the movement could so easily have advanced here as it developed in Glasgow under Charles Rennie Mackintosh.

69. Warehouses on Redcliffe Back – The Western Counties Co-operative Society Warehouse, *1896 by William Venn Gough*

Bristol has consistently turned its sourest and most industrial face to the riverside. The aesthetics of the 20th century have reversed the accepted taste of earlier centuries and the coarse angularity and rough textures of the riverside warehouses have become generally appreciated in Bristol, as in London, just at the time when they are being bought up for development. This range along Redcliffe Back is one of the last survivors of 19th-century commerce and the WCA warehouse is a particularly fortunate survivor not only for the aggressive confidence of its functional oriels, but because it is Bristol's first building in reinforced concrete.

70. Fairfield School, Fairfield Road, Montpelier, *1897 by William Larkins Bernard*

What Montpelier, one of Bristol's most rewarding suburbs, lacks is a church tower to pull it together as St Matthew's does to Kingsdown. Instead it has this towering confection of gables, more German than Jacobean, rising like the castle of a wicked margrave above the tangle of terraced houses. Bernard was primarily a school architect and this is easily his finest design, authoritative but full of colour and pattern, composing in a variety of ways because he has spent so much thought and invention on the lower supporting structures. It will be a tragedy if this is ever replaced by a bland piece of functionalism, for a school building's first function is to have character and this brims over with it.

71. Cabot Tower, Brandon Hill, *1897–8 by William Venn Gough*

With his feeling for drama at any price and his uninhibited eclecticism, Venn Gough was most safely employed when devising landmarks without any normal function. To experience the Cabot Tower it is not enough merely to acknowledge its prominence in the cityscape. It has to be climbed. A narrow winding stair, almost completely dark, leads to the stage of the four balconies, each one guarding its spectacular view until the last moment and then actually projecting the viewer over the void. Then comes another even narrower and darker stair as preliminary to the topmost parapet where the views are wider and unrationed, but there is still an elaboration of stonework, flying buttresses and Gothic arches rising even higher. Seen from below, the tower's profile is satisfying. The blank lower half is articulated by strong buttresses and the richness of the parapet and spire manages, by its sheer originality, to signal a secular image. No one ever supposes that there was once a church here as at Glastonbury. It is easy perhaps to mock, but entry is free and the tower records a level of civic confidence and prosperity that would be impossible to parallel in these reduced days.

72. City Museum and Art Gallery, Queen's Road, *1899–1904 by Sir Frank Wills*

As the 19th century drew to a close, Bristol became notably more prosperous, partly because people were smoking more cigarettes, and this is the city's tardy response to Liverpool's Walker Art Gallery, a status symbol donated by the Wills family and designed by one of them. Sir Frank was a large, genial man, capable of designing a most impressive Gothic church, St Andrew, Blagdon. But here he had to make a confident civic statement that would stand up to the former Museum and Library (**plate 42**) next door. His Museum works idiosyncratically on the street scene, not helped by being sited on a slope and rather deflated by the enormous tower of the Wills memorial building which Oatley added after 1914 and which, of course, Sir Frank could hardly have anticipated. On the debit side his elevation neither suggests art nor provides an obviously welcoming entrance. It was a perverse decision to make the great central projection into a cavernous *porte-cochère* as if only those visitors who drove up in a carriage were really wanted. Then with only three windows in such an expanse of ashlar, the building has an unpopulated air, accentuated by the absence of a visible door. With those reservations it is an impressively active elevation, as if a very fat man was demonstrating that his weight was no handicap. Sir Frank has taken a design that would have been ideal for a small garden pavilion or casino and made the classical features baroque by a giant projection of their scale. What was needed were more small elements like that central temple window to dramatise the size of it all by their contrast.

73. Former Prudential Building, 17 Clare Street, *1899 by Alfred Waterhouse*

Only the colour, a wonderful plummy terracotta, reminds you that here an old shocker of the High
Victorian is now sailing in serenely towards the harbour of Edwardian good taste. Gables from
Amsterdam of around 1630 are composed effortlessly with corner turrets from the Loire a hundred
years earlier to dramatise a corner site. The three-dimensionality of past decades remains,
memories of Pembroke College, Cambridge, Manchester Town Hall, Eaton Hall, but all subdued

74. Former Star Life Building, now Dominions House, St Augustine's Parade, *designed in 1898 by Arthur Blomfield Jackson*

One of the most stimulating and frustrating buildings in the city centre, Dominions House has neither top nor bottom, but what comes in between gives some idea of the wealth of detail and invention that was lost when only three of its intended six storeys were built. Bristol is not rich in Art Nouveau design and whereas the Art Nouveau of Everard's printing works in Broad Street (**plate 81**) crosses the Celtic with the Byzantine, Dominions House sandwiches the wonderfully louche French sinuosity of its first floor between a ground floor that appears originally to have been baroque and an aggressively Jacobean range of bow windows on the second floor. Above this a three-arched loggia flanked by cupolas was projected, the whole topped by a steep chateau-type roof. The fine quality of the stonework has been revealed by recent renovation and perhaps one day the shops at pavement level will respond to the fantasy façade above them.

---

now within a smooth skin of ornament: fruit, flowers, geometrical patterns, nothing figurative to distract the eye. The flow of forces at the base of the round turrets runs down playfully yet satisfyingly onto miniature pediments that pretend to be flattened by the weight. All so tightly put together that you feel the central stack could be used as a handle to pull the whole package off the street for transportation elsewhere. A perfect example of Bristol learning Pont Street good manners from London and a clear proof that old dogs can learn new tricks.

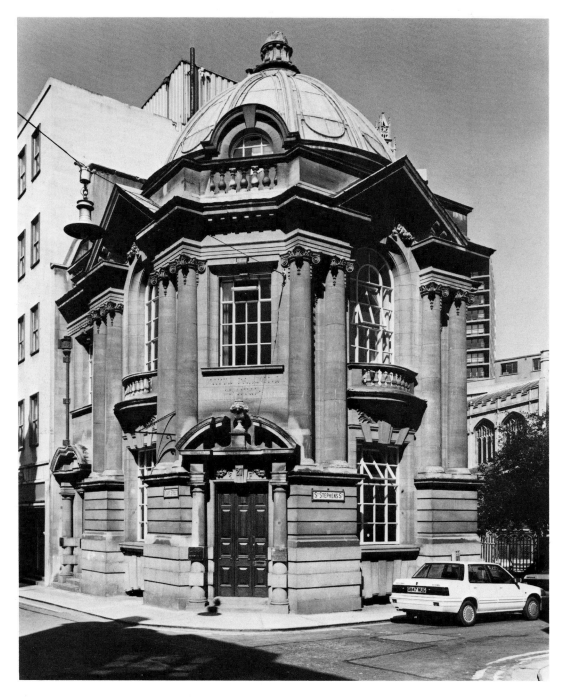

75. Scottish Provident Building, Clare Street, *1902–3 by Sir George Herbert Oatley and George Churchus Lawrence*

Does this owe more to the Radcliffe Camera at Oxford than to the domes of Austrian baroque? That the question needs to be asked proves that the building has its own stylistic identity, hard-edged and ruthlessly defined in every feature by slightly overplaying the scale of the ornament to the size of the dome. Arguably this is Bristol's best building by Sir Edwin Lutyens, who had nothing to do with it, and it makes again the point of Bristol's 19th-century self-sufficiency. As Foster and Wood kept George Gilbert Scott from the door, so there was no need for Lutyens to be commissioned when Oatley was at hand. The Scottish Provident should be compared with two others in the same street, E H Edwards's City Fire Office (**plate 57**) and Alfred Waterhouse's Prudential Building (**plate 73**), to see how a corner is turned with panache. Clearly the architects

76. Former Tramway Generating Station, now part of Courage's Brewery, Counterslip,
designed in 1899 by William Curtis Green

This is a magnificent Beaux Arts interloper on the Bristol quaysides, an import from the capital designed by a London-based architect. Its sheer quality may explain its survival to the present day when so many of the Bristol Byzantine warehouses which were once a common feature of the waterfront have been torn down. For one large rectangular box the Generating Station will repay a remarkably long examination as it has the unity and diversity of great architecture. One usual failing of the Beaux Arts is fussy detail and uncertain reference. Here Curtis Green broke through boldly to the more native line of 17th-century Baroque and 18th-century Palladian. The two great rows of arched windows to the riverside hint at the basement and first floor of a palace while never for a moment concealing the tough industrial function that the walls contain. With little fine detail a bold dramatic contrast is produced by the clash of Bath stone and pink brick, while the brick pilaster strips interrupted by a stone cornice, take up again in the next storey to pull the two floors together. Another unifying factor is the Ionic order, massive in detached columns to the street front, less insistent but still present on the longer sides of the building. On the street front the arched theme is also reinforced: first in the recessed and panelled arch of the lower floor window which offers and then denies an entry, and again in the great arched window which, quite incorrectly from a strict classical point of view, gives depth to the colonnade. It is due, in part at least, to this inspiring survivor from the old industrial order that so many of the office buildings which have gone up recently on the quaysides have been so rich, confident and various in their design.

---

were getting better, or the patrons more generous, all the time. Then come back to this last of the trio to enjoy, not just the art by which it concentrates your eye on the doorway so that you hardly notice a corner is being turned, but the dextrous diversity of levels – windows, string-courses, balconies, cornice and pediments – all seemingly ignoring each other's height and breaking rough imaginary lines, yet all pulling together into a coherent whole. If this were a Roman church it would be world famous; in Bristol's home-grown square mile it is merely standard.

77. Stock Exchange, St Nicholas Street, *1903 by Henry Williams*

Not many stock exchanges deserve to be described as 'pretty'. This one does. It is perhaps the most inappropriate building in Bristol. The marble columns suggest a high class bordello patronised by Ronald Firbank, the frieze is Adam, the windows are Barry and the porch is Laudian. Nothing hints at high finance except for the prodigality of a one-storey casino in an area of steep ground rents. It would be interesting to know the exact wording of Williams's commission. Was he given 'Gentlemen at Play' as a theme? The elevation offers an insight into why 'pastiche' is usually a derogatory term. The Exchange proves an inner vacancy in the man who designed it. Williams could have had no conviction, only cleverness; he was in fact a notable draughtsman. He seems to have observed the work of other men but never assimilated it. Like a number of his contemporaries he is playing games, waiting for the rude barbarians of the Bauhaus to batter at the gate with their superior urgency.

78. Stock Exchange – interior

The quirky but fastidiously detailed jumble of the Stock Exchange's exterior is a warning that inside anything could happen and here, in the main stairwell, Williams fulfils that threat. The mood now is Art Nouveau with those characteristic fat spade shapes imposed arbitrarily on the conventional curlicues of the stairs ironwork. Rich tulip tiles colour the walls beneath the dado rail and then, without warning, the upper walls burst into light-reflecting and light-creating ceramic tiles with a more delicate tulip motif. Functionally it is most successful in the way meagre light from a lantern set low amongst higher buildings is picked up and amplified. But the high gloss of it all and the scantily garbed nymph in her classical niche give the space more the air of a Turkish bath than a setting for stern financial dealings.

79. Former London and Lancashire Assurance Building, now Gateway Building Society, Corn Street, *1904 by Edward Gabriel*

To enjoy an average Bristol business house of the last great age a specialised aesthetic approach has to be developed, one very close to the way in which a church monument is appreciated. The elements of the façade are so tightly composed, often so disturbingly at war with each other and all piled so improbably one above the other, that the visual digestion can easily give up and the sheer verticality of the composition be rejected as un-English. In this elevation, for instance, all the features of a major country house, a Castle Howard even, have been crammed into three bays and five storeys. Only the baroque dome belongs naturally to a vertical unit, all the rest – rusticated

80. Shirehampton Public Hall, now also Library, *1903–4 by Frederick Bligh Bond*

It is by buildings such as this that the Edwardian period, though brief, achieves a distinct and separate identity. This has a sunny and confident eclecticism remote in spirit from the earnest and half-digested borrowings of the High Victorians. Symmetry and asymmetry are both firmly balanced; the hall is thoroughly three-dimensional and reveals new inventions on all sides with deep, spatial penetrations that never allow an elevation to become blank or tedious. If there is a basic stylistic identity it is that of Norman Shaw's ingenious version of 17th-century Surrey vernacular. The style depends upon colour contrasts of white paint with tile and brick – it is, therefore, particularly suited to the cheerful hues of the average red Pennant. Here Bligh Bond creates an almost seaside informality and approachable human scale. The spire of the clock tower behaves like a comical hat, and it becomes easy to see why later civic bureaucrats retreated behind the drab formalism of 'functional' buildings which would chill the visitor and inspire a baffled respect, as does Vincent Harris's Council House of 1935 on College Green. This Shirehampton Hall, in contrast, speaks with the ease and civilised perceptions of an early E M Forster novel.

---

basement, colonnade, entablature and segmental pediment – are associated with an easy horizontality spread across acres of grass and gravel. That is what sets the Victorians and Edwardians apart from the general spirit of English architecture. Only they and the Jacobeans had this passion for eating breakfast, lunch, tea and supper, all together in one meal. Social psychologists might explain such buildings, we have only to enjoy them. To set bows and cross-mullions between an Ionic giant order cannot be described as a solecism, more a functional exuberance; while Michaelangelesque figures perched on a segmental pediment, more usually internal than external features, make lively street furniture provided the street is pedestrianised and safe for upward-staring walkers. A last thought. Such a cheerfully uninhibited fashion of design would inevitably provoke a reaction and we have paid dearly for it ever since in puritanical functionalism.

82. Air Balloon Hill Council Schools, Hillside Road, *1905 by Latrobe and Weston*

Built of ash grey stone, snub, muted and faintly perverse in all its features, the complex of Infant School, Junior School and Manual Instruction Centre, is a perfect piece of civic aspiration in an enlightened industrial area at the turn of the century. It lies among the plain, adequate houses of the district like an extra-large set of Liberty-designed pewter ware. The Instruction Centre even has three sinuous Liberty-type roses carved on its gable end. Apart from one or two notionally Gothic windows, Latrobe and Weston have studiously avoided any reference to vernacular architecture or the picturesque. The grey, flaking Pennant walls are relieved by Bath stone bands with a strong horizontal emphasis and by squat, domed pylons at points of entry. Windows and doors are sometimes topped with a parabolic stone arch above a flat lintel, and the whole complex has been designed by architects touched by the Art Nouveau but inclining by nature towards a sturdy functionalism. The result is a rough, characterful poetry set in a suburb of the city that needed just that quality.

---

81. Everard's Printing Works, Broad Street, *1900 by Henry Williams; faience decoration by W J Neatby*

To understand this wholly enjoyable façade it is unprofitable to debate Celtic or Byzantine origins or weigh the Arts and Crafts movement against the Art Nouveau. All that is necessary is to follow the name of Morris, set there under the angel's wing on the first floor arcading. It was William Morris's *News From Nowhere* that inspired the jewel-like colours and the overt, loosely mediaeval cheerfulness of its iconography. Edward Everard was the true creative force behind his pliant architect and his willing tile-maker. He was evoking the vision of the future which Morris created where industry has become human in scale, deliberately decorative in its setting and in what it produced, where cities have become half-rural and the Spirit of Light, shaped like a rather threateningly sensual woman, presides over honest trade. Sadly, Bristol never took up Everard's challenge to link industry with art in everyday life. Perhaps he should have had Neatby set his faience decoration on a more acceptably English elevation, following the Gothic or baroque façades that had become standard over the last 50 years on Bristol's business houses. Instead he must have directed Henry Williams, who could follow any style with slavish competence, towards the Liberty designs then ultra-fashionable. Hence the jam-pot pinnacles, the flat, squashed hearts of beaten copper and the stylised flowers. This was the sophisticated face of Socialism.

83. Formerly The Wylands, High Street, Shirehampton, now a Telecom Engineering Department School, *1904 by Frederick Bligh Bond*

'Sweetness and Light' positively exude from this charming, even ingratiating house. This is Queen Anne classicism as it never existed in the 18th century but only in the last years of Victoria and the nine of Edward VII's reign. Bond has handled Richard Norman Shaw's revivalism with imagination. There is symmetry but never tedium. With its irregular formalities, two open pediments, one casually dramatising an oriel, its upper windows opening onto a generous balcony and the playful miniaturism of its attic dormers, the house has that flexibility which the Italianate had provided in the 1840s, but now everything is evocatively English. There is promise of log fires within or cucumber sandwiches on the lawn, dependent on the season. The detail of the eaves, florid at the corners and deeply shadowed in between, binds all the rambling elevations with a careless authority.

84. A-Bond Tobacco Warehouse, New Cut, *1905 by the building firm of Cowlings*

Appreciation here is very much an emotional and personal thing. A-Bond can be seen as a superb piece of brutalism, a significant shape lowering over steep banks of soft slime, honestly declaring the menace of lung cancer. Certainly some effort has been made to discipline the brute and make it logical. Darker brick both supports and defines the mass and the deep, four-bay central projection lends it an almost classical authority. Internally the two lower floors are carried on steel, the others on cast iron, but that hardly impacts on an outsider. Another way of looking at this trio of monsters is to compare them with the care, artifice and the expense that were poured into The Granary (**plate 41**) 36 years earlier. Surely, for the return on capital involved, the structures can fairly be balanced against each other? The merchant princes of Bristol have, as the 20th century opens, lost their way. From any one of a hundred viewpoints in the high-set city, the bonded warehouses are a depression to the spirit and an offence to a superb natural site. Only a perverse evaluation of abstract form protects them from civic outrage. Indeed, B-Bond is shortly to be the new home of the Bristol Record Office.

85. Former Western Congregational College, Cotham Road, now The Southern Universities Examinations Board, *1905–6 by Henry Dare Bryan*

With this butterfly-wing design Bryan demonstrated that to be successful a building does not have to arrive, it only has to divert, and this the Western College does abundantly. The great bay windows are far too large for the relatively short wings and hammer home the symmetry of the building without providing terminal features. Shrinking between turrets that suggest pepper-sprinkling rather than any stylistic period, the central gable is weak and recessed. But so much else is going on that a basic theme appears an irrelevance. The end walls are flirtaciously angled to reveal hyperactive but largely blank surfaces, the roofline bristles with minor incidents and anyone passing by along the pavement becomes visually involved with the steep, illogical batter of the scalloped courtyard walls. Bryan may have intended to suggest the point at which a Tudor country house side-stepped the Jacobean stage and tipped towards the Artisan Mannerist. That some kind of authentic historicism was on his mind is proven by an enchanting switch to half-timbered vernacular in the adjoining Principal's house around the corner. The College, Highbury Chapel, the Homeopathic Hospital and the return façade of a blousy late classical terrace are all set casually on a roundabout which occupies the site of the original Bristol gallows. A remarkable display of characterful but wholly discordant fine building.

86. Municipal Library, Deanery Road, *1906 by Charles Holden in partnership with Percy Adams and Lionel Pearson*

It is only from this south-eastern angle that the dual qualities of Holden's masterwork can be enjoyed: its angular symmetries and its amazing freedoms. This dualism is what makes the Library such an important and admired introduction to the Modern Movement. The south elevation, like the more often photographed north elevation to the main road, is so wilful in its complexities that the basic reassurance of its balanced discipline is easily overlooked. Instead the mind reacts to the sheer cliffs of ashlar above the absurdly low and aggressively jutting bow-oriels. Then it registers the Tudor mullions caught so inappropriately under round arches and between sleek, battered buttresses. Obviously a game is being played, Post-Modernism with all its cunning allusions to the past is alluding vigorously away even before the Modern Movement has become established. The Library is, in that sense, a wonderful confidence trick: the kind of modern building a traditionalist feels able to digest. But then on its east front or downhill helter skelter of volumes, when, facing the cathedral's disapproving towers, Holden might have been expected to be most cautious, he allows the interior functions and the exterior gradient to jostle the elevation into the Library's most satisfying freedoms. The staircase bulges its backside without concealment, basements multiply and the planes of the masonry recess exactly as and when they need. And yet – three carved shields, a blind arcading that can only be decorative but hangs isolated between defiant angularities – it is a structure of infinite, devious resources, an excitement to approach, an impossibility to define.

87. Wills No 1 Factory, Lombard Street & East Street, Bedminster, *1908 by Sir Frank Wills*

With the profits of the tobacco industry, a Beaux Arts factory in deep red terracotta was easily affordable. As its collieries were worked out, Bedminster became Bristol's closest approximation to a Lancashire mill town with a series of portentous elevations, all by Sir Frank and dating from 1884 onwards, rising along one side of the main shopping street. Even now when part has been demolished and the Gothic block visible on the right of this photograph has been turned into a

88. Former Vandyck Press, now Bristol University Drama Department, Park Row, *1911 by Mowbray Aston Green*

If you look very carefully at this frowning cliff of rough-hewn purple Pennant stone there are just one or two hints at what the architect was trying to express – the batter in the lower walls that dramatises those two entries on the right, the simple solidity of the ironwork and that one coy, bulls-eye window with its architrave of smoother stone. Otherwise there are no more clues to the fact that Mr Mowbray Green, a most sensitive enthusiast for Georgian classicism, was putting on his gruffest voice and giving Bristol an Arts and Crafts business premise so uncompromising that very few people notice it. The essence of the Arts and Crafts was to let the materials express themselves, hence an essay in purple Pennant and heavy iron. But to allow materials to speak clearly it is necessary to project them by tough asymmetries and that Mowbray Green, with his classical training refused to do. Only in the lower right-hand corner does his syntax become a shade contorted and therefore interesting. Given its steep hillside site this could have been the city's equivalent of the Glasgow School of Art, the Mackintosh masterpiece. Five years later with Charles Holden's Municipal Library (**plate 86**) to give him courage, Mowbray Green might have broken the Vandyck's roofline and allowed the fenestration to vary with the internal spaces; instead Park Row got a very deep growl from Pooh Bear.

---

shopping mall, the effect is formidable. For his two main street elevations the architect has achieved a severe geometry with a mix of Doric pilasters and Tuscan columns. When he came to that ever taxing problem of turning a corner with courage his invention held for the three upper floors – grand Venetian oriel, coupled Tuscan columns and the comical hat of the dome. For the entrance door, however, which did not have to be sited at this vulnerable point, he copied E H Edwards's unhappy device of 1889 in the City Fire Office (**plate 57**), undercutting the oriel and the whole corner with a sagging support of scrollwork and cartouche.

89. Fountain and Statue of Edward VII, Victoria Rooms, Queen's Road, Clifton, *fountain of 1912 by Edwin Alfred Rickards and Henry Poole; statue of 1913 by Poole*

As Charles Dyer first designed them, the steps up to the Victoria Rooms were only as wide as the portico and were flanked by sphinxes. But in 1907 Poole and Rickards, who had been working very successfully together at Cardiff City Hall, won a competition to give the Rooms an Edwardian touch of florid civic grandeur. So the fountain with the two lions replaced the sphinxes on a much wider flight of steps in 1912. Poole's statue of the King was added in 1913. This explains why the King in coronation robes (the only respectable way Poole could introduce a show of leg into his sculpture) is not dressed appropriately for the highly inventive group of mermen, crustaceans, seaweed and an octopus revelling in the waters below him. The two were not intended as a unit though there is a hint of Art Nouveau sinuosity to both.

90. Royal Empire Society, Whiteladies Road

Something very strange has been going on in the design of this interesting composite creation. A date of 1921 has been offered for it, which would place it outside the limits of this book, but it has also been suggested that an earlier 19th-century building was adapted and included. That would appear to be the angled façade on the right with its elevated Venetian window. As for the main façade with its remarkable bow window formed from a semi-circular Corinthian temple, this is Edwardian in spirit if not in building date. With its Atlantides wearily shouldering the great burden of a global empire (the series continues out of sight around the corner) the elevation perfectly captures that Kiplingesque vision of an immense labour gallantly supported by an impartial master-race destined to administer peace and justice to 'the lesser breeds without the Law'.

Index to the Plates